GiVE ME BacK MY Crayons

Give Me Back My Crayons

10 Keys to Unlocking the Creative Child Within

JoAnn Nocera

inspired girl BOOKS

For Gregory and Gerard Philip, may you always
keep the creative spirit alive and never forget
you are a gift to this world.

Advanced Praise

"JoAnn Nocera approaches life and her life's work—education—with a passion and positivity that is infectious and which is echoed in the hallways of her school building. Having worked with her on several initiatives, I know her to be innovative and open-minded, someone whose dedication to art-infused education has fostered a learning environment that is inclusive, experiential, collaborative, and which generates positive results. JoAnn is proof that joy is not superfluous to a quality education, but integral."

Mike Kenny, Toms River Regional Schools

"JoAnn is a 'creative force!' I have known and worked creatively with JoAnn for five years and have witnessed her love and intensity for art! She inspires and continues to grow the love for art education and to deepen the true spirit of creativity. As Albert Einstein said, 'Creativity is contagious. Pass it on.' JoAnn is contagious with her love and passion for being creative, heart and soul, and passing it on!"

Karen Pomeroy, Art Teacher

"In life there is always someone who inspires you, challenges you, and encourages you to achieve your goals. JoAnn Nocera is one of those great educators who does just that. I had the wonderful privilege of working with JoAnn as the Media/ Technology Specialist. JoAnn has an energetic personality and she continually helps her students and staff to follow their dreams."

Helen Koerner, Librarian and Media Specialist

"JoAnn Nocera is the epitome of what a teacher should be in today's world. She possesses a passion, dedication and love for her students that is second to none, and it is easily seen in the excitement her students display. I have known JoAnn since my son was a student in her class over 10 years ago, and to see the love, reverence, and respect that he and his classmates still have for her is a testament to how special she is."

Robert LoPresti, Parent

"I've known JoAnn Nocera for more than 10 years as an extraordinary professional. In the classroom she is a dynamo, partnering with other educators, seeking professional development from the arts to opportunities with NASA. As a supervisor, she has built a culture of caring and collaboration, sharing all of her Crayons with anyone who might be interested . . . because as soon as they give it a try, they are all in! Her creativity has inspired families to engage in their children's learning process and children to find their inner artist and a means of expressing it through multimedia, multicultural learning experiences."

Tiffany Lucey, Supervisor of Educational Technology

Foreword

by Janelle Leonard

What is creativity?

Is it gone from our homes and schools?

"Mrs. Leonard, you're in charge." Those words greeted me as twenty fifth graders were ushered into the library. A few of them brought books to read, but the others stared expectantly at me. What were they supposed to do for an hour?

So, to keep them distracted from climbing bookshelves or the trees decorating the corners, I grabbed paper, crayons, glue, safety scissors, and of course, googly eyes. I set them on the tables and said, "Have fun!"

They grabbed at the supplies like marbles in a Hungry Hungry Hippos game. Silliness ensued as they drew odd shaped horses, attached huge googly eyes to stick figures, traced their faces, and cut out butterflies. Laughter filled the library as well as wonderful masterpieces that I hung on a clothesline on my art wall.

Several of the boys took it even further, asking, "Can we make bookmarks to put in books around the library?" Over the next couple days, students in all grades were delighted to find a googly eye peering over the pages at them—excited that they could keep the handmade bookmark. That creative day sparked the bug in others and every day I receive perfectly, imperfect drawings and creations.

This is the type of scene JoAnn has painted in her book *Give Me Back My Crayons*. She's provided the tools, excitement, fun, and a judgment-free environment to unlock the creative child within yourself and those around you.

I've had the privilege of meeting JoAnn through the pages of this book. In her I've found a kindred spirit. A lover of creativity who is passionate about seeing children's (and adult's) eyes light up as they create unabashedly. With her stories and creativity cues, JoAnn graciously reminded me about the precious moments I've created, that it's okay to be messy, to enjoy the process, to be present not perfect, and that it's wonderfully freeing to be your unique self.

Within these pages, you'll find a friend, a creativity advocate, and mentor. You'll discover a message that will undeniably unlock the creative child within. Whether you read this in one sitting or in the spare moments between school hours, naps, and bedtime—come open. Come excited. Come expectant.

Come with a box of crayons, ready to color your life's masterpiece!

Introduction

I remember when I got my first box of crayons, it was like opening presents on Christmas morning. Each color gifted me ideas and sparked my imagination.

Pure joy!

I often wondered though, why didn't they group similar colors together? Who made the executive decision to specify groupings in a box of 64? How did they decide which colors to add? Creativity does that, you know. It makes you think, it makes you question the world . . . it makes you find answers to situations and look at the world in a different way.

Sometimes it takes a lifetime to realize that creativity is inside us all, we were just too busy to give it the time to take shape or the opportunity to rear its head without us suppressing it. More often than not, children and adults are put in situations where they feel there is a right or wrong way to approach learning. They give up their gut instinct because they're afraid of failure, of "doing it wrong."

I was a maker for most of my life, moving beyond just

crayons to all forms of making—from needle and thread to watercolor to cardboard to poetry. And when I started teaching, over 20 years ago, oh how I loved infusing the arts into basic subjects like reading, science, math, and social studies. The children came alive and dove into the subject matter when they were asked to create a piece around it. Magical, really.

But with the dawn of technology, budgets that went to art supplies were allocated to machines, and curriculums were based around standardized tests leaving little room for art in the classroom.

Without creativity, we lose our sense of curiosity. We no longer trust our intuition, and as a result, so many children wait passively for others to tell them what to do, how to think, and what colors to use.

Why are children afraid to question their world around them and be solution-driven instead of accepting what is? How could a child be courageous to think creatively when the message is clear that learning is fact gathering, only to regurgitate it back through a worksheet or assessment?

I ask these questions, but I know the answers.

So many times I just wanted to scream, "Give Me Back My Crayons!" I longed to bring that magic back into their eyes, return the spark for learning to their hearts.

And so, I set out to infuse arts into learning both at school and with parents at home. As a school administrator supported by an incredible, like-minded team, I've spent the better part of the last decade doing just that in my school and creating a *Parent Academy* to encourage creativity to continue in the home.

I hope this book brings you the courage to take time for yourself and your children to tap into your creative spirit. Chapters will cover how we look at creativity in the home and the classroom, as well as the mindsets and language used around creativity. The book reveals obstacles that can get in the way of our "making" and developing a creative life. Creativity is an entry point for so many students who can't see their way to the academics void of any art form. Please feel free to interact with each chapter and share on my social media community (once the "making" is done).

At the end of each chapter I've placed "Creative Cues." These are ideas to help place creativity in your life. To give your creative spirit the chance to show itself. To place you in a better place each and every day with yourself emotionally and spiritually.

It's time for creativity to take its place in our world! It's time to recapture and recreate that feeling of opening that first box of crayons!

Love and blessings for a beautiful life ahead.

CREATIVITY
[ˌkrēāˈtivədē]

NOUN

the use of the imagination or original ideas, especially in the production of an artistic work.

"firms are keen to encourage creativity"

synonyms:

inventiveness · imagination · imaginativeness · innovation · innovativeness · originality · individuality · artistry · expressiveness · inspiration · vision · creative power · creative talent · creative gift · creative skill · resourcefulness · ingenuity · enterprise

KEY #1:

CELEBRATE YOUR UNIQUE SELF

You Are Amazing As You Are

"You are BRAVER than you believe,
STRONGER than you seem,
SMARTER than you think and
LOVED more than you'll ever know."
~ A.A. Milne

Growing up, I was blessed to have both grandmothers alive until I was in High School. My maternal grandmother lived in an apartment downstairs and was bound to a wheelchair. She'd broken her hip and never recovered fully, and had the onset of Parkinson's Disease. I didn't know about this until I was older. I just accepted the disability because she was my loving grandmother. My family didn't focus on the illness, we just strived to make each day count in the best way possible.

She told me stories of her sewing machine and the beautiful cabinet that hid it away. When my grandmother talked about it, my grandfather happily went over to the cabinet and showed me how the Singer machine would "pop-up" from its space below and perfectly set itself. They showed me how to thread the needle and where the bobbin would nestle itself inside. When my Grandmother's hands shook and she grew frustrated, my grandfather would step in. It amazed me that he knew how to thread a needle.

When I was about 8 or 9, I decided to clean out the notions drawer in her sewing table. It was like finding little surprises. Lace wrapped around a faded piece of cardboard. Buttons galore in all shapes and sizes, one more ornate than the next. Zippers, big and small. Little hook & eyes.

I remember asking, "What are these for?" With each new treasure I found, I had more questions and became more curious. They were amused by my curiosity, but patiently answered all my inquiries.

Oh, how close we all were. Close and always creating something, because that's just the way the world was. I remember my mother making a blanket for my brother in anticipation of his birth. We talked as she crocheted strips, attaching them together to form one large blanket. Design and construction modeled for me . . . what a thrill.

As I continued to watch my grandmother and Mom, I realized I had an interest. I'd take worn-out clothing and change them into something new. I still have a pouch made from a leg of an old pair of jeans. My embroidery stitches were random and unpolished, but they were mine. I never compared or questioned my work, I just continued to practice hand sewing.

My earliest memory of creativity at school was finger painting in Kindergarten. It didn't bother me that it was all messy and wet. I enjoyed watching the colors mix and emerge as a new one on the paper. For some reason I remember coloring books and crayons were the treats given as a take home gifts after a birthday party. I had a collection of coloring books, and I'd rip out pages to hang up and give as gifts.

At home my experiences were drawing, sewing and trying out a loom. The loom was a plastic cylinder shape that would create a long string, like an enlarged shoelace. I used it to attach to a fabric bag or sewed them together to make potholders and bowls.

By the time I was in high school I was electing to take every and any art class. Fashion design became a focus and I couldn't wait to buy the *New York Times* on a Sunday. This enormous paper would have full spread drawings of fashion figures from Lord & Taylor and at a certain time of year, the *New York Times* included a fashion magazine in one of their Sunday papers. I anticipated and begged my parents to buy the Sunday paper, especially on that day. My fashion design teacher, Mrs. Rose, expected me to put together a fashion design portfolio for F.I.T., but I never had the courage to move in that direction.

Uncreative Detour

All my silly enthusiasm and energy came to an end when high school hit and a decision had to be made for the future. How can art bring in any kind of income? Fashion class? While that'd be fun, it wasn't accepted as a real career.

Nurse?

Secretary?

"You're just going to get married and have kids," I heard from friends and family. "Pick a career that will help see that through."

I'd always dreamed of being a teacher. My childhood friends pretended to be my students as I taught them on the concrete sidewalk on hot summer days. I gave them stickers and happily made marks of "Excellent!" on their papers. My parents even bought me a chalkboard on wheels. I spent many days teaching my illiterate grandparents—who only made it to 8th grade before they had to go to work to bring in money for their families—words and grammar rules.

My dad wanted my siblings and me to graduate from college, but when the time came my choices were limited. It was a difficult decision, but being swayed by the social norms of having money and materialistic items drove me in a direction that would become my hardest hurdle.

I ended up at a two-year secretarial school. After graduating, I began my working life at J. Aaron, a subsidiary of Goldman Sachs. For years my creativity was suppressed by the routine of the trading floor and the serious world of finance.

I left Goldman Sachs because I was pregnant with Gregory. My coworkers and colleagues told me to get a nanny. All the traders I worked with had apartments in the city and had nanny's and au pairs. But I didn't want to pay someone to raise my son. They thought I was crazy when I left the company to be a stay-at-home Mom. I knew this was the right decision for me. During this time, I decided to go back to school and fulfill my dreams of being a teacher. The next eleven years I made up for lost time. I finished my education and obtained my teaching license. I never looked back and knew in my heart it was the right decision for my family and myself.

You see, after I had children I realized my creativity couldn't be contained. I knew I was different and that I saw the world through an artist's eye. My need to be in museums and around studios was always tugging at my heart. I found classes for myself and even signed up my boys when they were little to see if they had a love for creativity like I did.

I had so much fun with my boys! Birthday parties were a time for creativity and joy. It came easy to me because I paired everything with story book characters or fairy-tale legends. Everything from costumes to cupcakes and somehow the Polaroid camera was like a photo booth of today.

When we had a pirate party, everyone had eye patches and bandanas and we had to find the treasure of gold coins and prizes. During a circus party, the kids walked the tightrope on the deck with an umbrella. We painted faces and wore silly costumes. I made clowns from soda bottles and put some marbles at the bottom. The kids had to knock the clowns down, like a carnival. We sang songs, pretended, and laughed.

Friends would ask me how I was so creative. I can only believe it is because of those who inspired me to unlock the creativity within me. My grandparents, parents, and teacher's journey wasn't to convince others or me to be creative, but their love and passion led me to take a chance and immerse myself into their world. By doing so, I gathered many skills and talents that make up who I am today—a plethora of experiences not in one area but a multitude.

And like those who inspired me, my hope is not to convince you to be creative, but rather make you aware that you already are.

Celebrating YOU!

Now I'm talking to you—not as a parent—JUST YOU!! When was the last time you put on a party hat and celebrated YOU? This chapter is dedicated to YOU the reader because we often lose ourselves in life. We get lost to sports teams, music lessons, drive through meals, taking care of everyone and everything except ourselves.

Life gives us mixed messages. Work hard, raise star children, strive for perfection in yourself and family—or close to it. We are all over-worked, over-scheduled and pressures of parenting leave little room for JOY.

During the years of raising my children, working full-time and trying to work at fixing a failed marriage left little time for me. I didn't give myself the time to nurture me. I pushed down and away the time for making. If it did surface for a month I would attend to it and then put it away as if it was a waste of time or frivolous.

My cabinets were filled with supplies of all kinds waiting to be used. Scrapbooking papers and tools, watercolor paints brushes, and paper, pastels, acrylic paints and canvases. You name it, I had it. Jumping from one medium to another and investing in everything to go with it. Waiting for it to have a place in my life.

I would buy in full force to show I was committing to the process but then lay it to rest as my life pulled me away. There were games to attend and papers to grade. There were meals to be cooked and laundry to be done. There never seems enough time to do the things you want to do. I never regretted attending those games and being present in my children's lives. I loved every moment, but I was lacking a balance.

It was unfortunate that it took tremendous pain for me to find my creative self again.

All the creative experiences of my childhood and past held the key to my happy place. It didn't matter if I was painting, sewing, knitting, cooking, embroidering, quilting . . . I was "making." I was taking the colors of yarn, thread, fabric and piecing them together in a way I couldn't imagine would heal me of my tremendous pain. Somehow the brokenness was healed through using my hands to create the most adorable little baby cardigans that were knit with beautiful soft wool. Quilted scraps of fabric to make wall hangings. Squares of different knitted patterns to make blankets.

I studied fashion design in high school and so much of my artwork reflects that. Drawings and watercolor paintings too. Then there were perspective drawings. I guess that was the curriculum for 7th grade students. But I took it a step further. My drawings became beach scenes that were fixed in a pastel picture that I would turn to when I needed to be hopeful. Why were there so many pictures of pathways during my married life? Maybe my art was a reflection of my heart. Where would the path take me if I could leave this place of pain? What lies on the other side of this beautiful trail? I made a pastel drawing of a beach path that still hangs in my house today. It has so much meaning to me—a symbol of my freedom.

Freedom to be me. Freedom to open myself up to the possibilities of what lies beyond the safe walls I built around myself. Freedom to create.

Can art give us insight into our future or reflect who we will become if we let it? If we let it, do we give ourselves, our creative selves a chance to shine?

Happiness and joy are the result when we trust the process. If we could just trust our inner self and not someone else's version, we will find our creative spirit. I truly believe the answer lies within each of us. We all have special talents to share with the world, but if we don't give ourselves the permission to let it out or tap into it, then it will be gone forever and the world will suffer for it.

Celebrate yourself.

Don't be afraid to acknowledge all the small steps you are taking to accomplish your goals. It doesn't have to be grandiose it can be as little as acknowledging something you said to another person that lifted them up or how you helped yourself get through a situation.

Keeping a journal of your small steps will help you see that everything is worth all the work and perseverance you put into it! When I was a teacher, I had to be aware of what children did and did not do in terms of achievement.

Goals were a major part of my student's journey in that grade level. What do you want to work on or improve in yourself and your academic ability? Students in my class would set reading goals by writing them and making them real. Some had charts to help them keep track of their growth in reading levels and math. Knowing they were making a public affirmation that they were continuing to grow and work toward getting better academically and emotionally made them take a vested interest in keeping to meeting their goal.

It's not too late for you to clear the plate of all that's weighing you down and focus on YOU! Yes, you will need to find quiet time even if it's for 10 min. Silently be with yourself and remove all thoughts of the busy day and the tug of the kids. Silently think about YOU.

The famous saying "Actions speak louder than words" is true in working toward a goal. Words can be so destructive.

If you feel the need to blurt out unkind words, stop and think how that might set a person back emotionally. Nothing is gained by this negativity.

Relax and if it's tiring you, just celebrate what's in the moment. What is happening right now in your life that you can celebrate? I know you are tempted to criticize or judge yourself or your situation but STOP yourself right here.

Own your imperfect day or life.

Somewhere in all the messiness there is a spark of JOY. A spark that left unnoticed will burn out and die. But if we consciously see the spark in ourselves and others, we can continue to have that JOY even in our imperfect days. Don't allow people to dim your light. You were made UNIQUE, no other person can be YOU!

Not only attending to being mindful even when our minds are full, but being aware of our physical health. According to a joint survey done by *Healthy Women* and *Working Mother*, 78% of moms report they put off taking care of their own health because they are too busy looking after their loved ones. Self-care is not an indulgence, it's a necessity. Self-care is simply making time to take care of your body so it can take care of you.

YOU ARE WORTH IT!

I know it might be hard to find joy in your journey, even when you can't see your way through unchartered territory. Joyful thoughts will help you start to clear away the fogginess and rest assured you will be heading in the right direction. Slow down and savor the small moments of success within yourself and others. Focusing on the positive will dim the negative.

Parent Academy

You will read about *Parent Academy* at different points in this book. *Parent Academy* is a group that provides support academically and emotionally to parents as they help educate their child in today's world. We hold workshops every month; each month is centered around different themes, and we invite parents and students in for a night of fun and learning! It was formed by teachers and administration in my school district who wanted to bring parents into the learning process. Our PTO also supports *Parent Academy* with funding to run these monthly workshops by providing the supplies we need and food to nourish us after a long day's work.

Modeling Unique Self at School

Teachers hold so much power in creating a classroom environment that embraces diversity. A classroom that nurtures everyone's spirit and holds true to the value of hard work, creativity, and grit will yield confident students who will have the strength to let their creative spirit connect to their work.

Encouraging talk might be, "Your writing has so many interesting details I can't wait to read more."

"This group is working together so nicely. I'm so happy to see each of you sharing your ideas and suggestions."

Modeling Unique Self at Home

Parents have a wonderful opportunity to model their acceptance of themselves and celebrate their uniqueness. We all have gifts and talents to share with the world. Those talents cannot be hidden or disguised because it will always surface. The more we push it away and ignore it the more unhappy we become because it is a part of us and cannot be taken away. We should be communicating to our children words that help them see that they are unique. For example, if your child shows signs of interest or passion in the arts, then support them by seeking programs or giving them experiences within that area. There are so many free programs in surrounding towns and cities that will introduce and help your child tap into their talents.

Creative Cues

Daily Affirmations

Find one thing each day to celebrate. Get up in the morning and face yourself in the mirror. Don't be afraid to say what's on your mind: "This presentation is making me feel nervous and unsure, but you've got this! You've prepared for weeks, you're all set with the handouts, and the slide presentation is ready to go! You worked hard ... YOU'VE GOT THIS!!" Sometimes saying affirmations out loud will go a long way in realizing that our minds make things bigger than they are. Don't let your negative thoughts get the best of you. You have the power to rise above any situation.

Celebration Dance

Create a celebration dance that's all yours. Find your favorite song or artist either on Pandora or Spotify or maybe there's a favorite feed that plays all your favorite artists. Blast it and start dancing. Yes, just dance! Move your body and feel the joy as you pay attention to the song and how the rhythm matches your moves. Don't think about anything but moving. Fist pump and jump several times at the end of the song. Then slowly stretch and sway, collapsing with complete Ahhhhhhh! Your body will love it.

Gratitude Journal

Keeping a journal to write down your thoughts and actions can help you set your goals into action. Celebrations are the end result of hard work whether it's regarding schoolwork or relationships. Find one thing or person you are grateful for and jot it down in your gratitude journal. It's amazing what reflection journals can do to help you be mindful of others and their actions. It's easy to slip into taking a person for granted and thinking that the big and little things they do for you will always be there. Think again, gratitude heals all hearts and wounds.

Celebrating Others

Find something in another person to celebrate. It's never too late to share kind words and thankful praises. Sometimes we get so caught up with our own lives and raising our children that we forget to stop and celebrate others. Whether we are in school, at home or at the store, you can always find opportunities to celebrate what others are doing . . . holding the door, bagging up your groceries, or even a friend who has gone out of their way for you or your child. This is a perfect opportunity to write your dear friend a handwritten note or pick up the phone and let them know you appreciate them. Handwritten notes and cards are a wonderful way to show that special someone you truly appreciate their gifts. Taking the time to show you care will help grow your relationship.

CREATIVITY BREAK

Think about who YOU are as a human being. Use the space below to write words or draw symbols that describe YOU. Be creative and have fun—open yourself up to the person you were born to be, not just who you are in this moment.

KEY #2

BE PRESENT

Not Perfect

"When you aim for perfection,
you discover it's a moving target."
~ *Geoffrey F. Fischer*

As teachers and administration come together each summer for a planning meeting, it was evident that a lot of the discussion that summer focused on the outdoor area of the building. There was a memorial garden dedicated to a former Special Education teacher full of weeds and unattended. Throughout the years, teachers maintained it but as the years passed, teachers could no longer do the manual labor. The administration wanted the planning committee to find a way to raise money to keep it as a place of dedication on our school grounds.

That initiative led to another discussion about the entrance of the building and how the staff would like to see flowers and landscaping. We formed a committee and started working together to get vines pulled out and mulch put in place around the front of the building. Teachers planned monthly fundraising events and called the group the Renovation Committee. They were set on updating the 60-year-old building. The district was so supportive to send Building and Grounds workers. They provided the mulch and removed vines. The district also supplied paint and the teachers and administrators painted a fresh coat on the walls in the main lobby. Slowly, new projects and updates were happening.

The fence at the entrance of the school was an old chain-link fence. The teachers talked about ideas to replace it. How can we embellish a garden and give it a fresh look? How can we involve the parents, students, and community? My mind started to think about fencing companies and if they would donate to our cause. Wooden pickets? Could the students paint them? With their parents?

Painting led me to connect my thoughts to our art show. Parents and students could engage in a creative activity that would bring them together away from the routines. Instead of holding their phones, they could hold a paintbrush.

I reached out to fencing companies and they were happy to donate the picket fences. After receiving 100 stray pickets that were left over from jobs, I primed them outside the building and they were ready to be painted. The committee met to work out the details of the paint, brushes, paper plates to act as a palette, and the idea took off. Creative thoughts sometimes take you on a path and you can't see where you're going, but you have to trust the process and each other. Like clay, creativity allows you to change and adapt until your make a masterpiece. Even if some parts crack and harden, the masterpiece still remains.

For those parents who showed up at the art show to paint with their children, they committed themselves to a night of being present. The families gathered together, talked about their ideas to paint the picket fence, and laughed and talked to each other throughout the whole process. There were no distractions away from their "making." They enjoyed each other's company because they gave into the creativity with no expectations of perfection. There were, however, parents who had a little insecurity of the final product and used their phones to Google pictures of picket fences and ideas for their project. This led to everyone in the family arguing, trying to decide which picture would be "perfect" to display their families efforts. The project took on a competitive feel as they looked around the room constantly to compare their work to others.

Perfection

Perfection is all around us. Oh how we all pay close attention to details. Critiquing everything from storefronts and window displays to color coordinating every room in every house, in every office—even classrooms. Not only is society coming down hard on themselves, but the expectations of others to be perfect . . . for children to be more knowledgeable, more accomplished, more polished at a younger and younger age.

New Scientist Magazine stated that, "Perfectionism can lead to mental health problems such as eating disorders, depression, anxiety and even suicide."

The worrisome part for me is that I've seen firsthand hundreds of students not even trying to help themselves for fear of failure and judgement from others. So they take a passive role in living and in learning. It is easier to seek help instead of digging deep into their intuition and persevere through the discomfort of learning something new whether it be in school or at home.

For example, let's take a Kindergarten student and ask them to tie their shoe. Some stick with the task that might take days and sometimes children immediately cry or get upset after the first try. Parents often lose their patience and give into buying Velcro shoes so tying a shoe doesn't slow down their routines and days. Manufacturers of toys had tying a shoe or buttoning up as part of a Sesame Street character doll in an effort to help children do something as simple as tying a shoe.

Shoe tying and practicing zippers and buttons had a place in New York City Public schools in the 70s. You could find those life skills in kindergarten classrooms years ago. They have vanished. Instead there are children in Kindergarten expected to use their fine motor skills to write letters, numbers, and sentences.

Happily there still exists play areas such as kitchens and

sand tables. It takes a tremendous amount of effort for teachers and parents today to fit in all the academic, social and emotional learning needed in those younger grades. Being present during huge learning growth requires all the patience a person or child needs to have with themselves and others. Trusting that the work will be difficult but somehow will see the light at the end of the tunnel. Perfection doesn't have a place when new learning is at hand.

Relieving yourself of the expectations of perfection opens the door to new and exciting learning opportunities. Creative thinking can be released and true ideas and innovation can emerge.

Truly Present

What does it take to be truly present?

By definition being truly present means having your focus, your attention, your thoughts and feelings all fixed on the task at hand.

It is difficult in today's world to be truly present because we are multitasking. The phone is ringing, the kids need to do their homework, and if you have more than one, you're jumping around helping each one of them get started. Or you're moving them through the task to get finished only to scoop them up and put them in the car to drive them to sports, dance, religious education class or music lessons all while monitoring conversation, music, and sibling rivalry.

Multitasking is the act of doing multiple things at once. For many, multitasking is more efficient than focusing on one task at a time. Studies have been carried out, and although some say that multitasking is an effective way to utilize time, the results of breaking off our attention into different tasks makes the quality of the work drop significantly.

Clifford Nass, a psychology professor at Stanford University has identified that when we multitask non-stop we actually waste more time. He also has reported that it may be killing our concentration and creativity too. Nass states that, "people who multitask all the time can't filter out irrelevancy. They can't manage a working memory. They're chronically distracted." The myth lies in thinking that we are more productive when in fact it debilitates us from completing one task well.

Additionally, Rene Marois at Vanderbilt University, published in December in the journal Neuron, found that our brains have difficulty concentrating fully on more than one task; "Multitasking involves dividing one's attention between the tasks, and because each task competes for a limited amount of cognitive resources, the performance of one interferes with that of the other. The greater the similarity of the tasks, the more interference there is, but there is also interference between completely dissimilar tasks."

When I think about the demands we put on ourselves while multitasking . . . take for example when we drive and talk on the phone whether it's hands free or not it's very distracting. The brain needs to have one of those actions the "primary focus," let's say that's the phone conversation, the driving then becomes the secondary focus and our brains will pay attention to the road here and there when it wants to. Now add the radio and other features on the dashboard as we are driving.

To be present then can actually be helpful and healing to our bodies and our minds. This chapter is not about being present with your children but finding and giving yourself the time to fully engage with the task at hand. Time for you to rethink the demands and the "irrelevancy" discussed about and be . . . just be in the moment with what you set out to do.

I realized this when I was two years into my teaching. The class consisted of twenty-five bright, articulate second grade students. Their ideas and imagination flowed. Each day we took learning to new heights. I could introduce works of art by Van Gogh and other famous artists. I would display a laminated poster of a famous piece of art and they would have opportunities throughout the school day to respond to it and add their thoughts and feelings about it.

Every subject was infused with art. I found an outline of Van Gogh's "The Church of Auvers." I kept it on an easel in the back of the room and students were encouraged to take their crayons and with quick small strokes fill up the paper with color. This class picture still hangs in my home today.

During the holidays, we pretended to take a trip around the world. We gathered information about culture, geography and each country's celebrations. Learning about the world and the differences that exist helped us appreciate each other's differences.

Confident and Proud

Do we sometimes question our decisions? Look to our friends and family for approval or permission?

It starts early in life when we experience situations that make us doubt who we are. Sometimes we can't always recognize the beauty and creativity that lies within us. Creativity resides in all of us but are we able to be true to it and see it as part of who we are however quirky we might think it is?

Let's go back to our childhood days. When we were children, did others help us to feel confident and proud in our creativity? What moment in your childhood turned you away from trusting your inner talents? In schools today we encourage deeper conversations. It's not enough to say, "great job."

When children are trying to reach a goal—short or long term it is going to require lots of conversation during each step along the way. They will need our guidance, but certainly we cannot take over their work and effort. Sometimes they need us to let them have space in which to figure it out. We need to appreciate their effort, communicating that along the way. They will need our reassurance that if the first time didn't give them the results they wanted, that it's okay to try it again and again. It will be tempting to just throw in the towel and move on, but then the message delivered to them is that we don't have confidence in them enough to see it through.

Focused

Before beginning an activity or diving into a new learning experience, I asked my students to breathe. Take in a breath and remove all distractions. Focusing on ourselves and our children takes practice. We need to give each other enough time to complete our work for that portion and time to give ourselves a break. Not multitasking and thinking about answering emails, texts, and changing the song all at the same time.

For my younger son, I would set a timer on the stove when he was working on either homework or a project. Building in breaks allowed him to get up and stretch his legs and move his body which activated his brain. Keeping focused means finding a balance of reasonable time to work and to take breaks.

Connected

We all want to feel connected to something—our families, our friends, school events, and groups outside of school. What makes us feel connected? Is it that we are visible and others can hear our thoughts and ideas when we express them?

Children need us to encourage them to open up. We don't have to have a solution for them but we can start by listening. Having the *Parent Academy* events has truly made so many children and their families feel connected to the school and the community. Relationships can easily be fostered when conversations go beyond the surface level.

At a very early age children are exposed to what and how things should be. Following directions is important to move the lessons along but when it comes to having the student communicate their learning back to the teacher, creativity can rear its head.

For example, if a student is learning about a time period or famous person, they can relay their learning in a different format other than a book report with a decorative cover. They can write a poem, song, create a mobile of information, a PowerPoint presentation and other possible products that aligns with their intelligences and learning style.

My friend recently told me a story about her son when he was in Kindergarten. The teacher asked him to make a bear using the paper given to him and the step-by-step directions on the board. He had to practice his gross motor skills and fine motor skills by cutting, tracing and gluing the pieces of paper together. Her son insisted that his bear needed to be green. He begged the teacher for green paper and he began to make his bear. He not only changed the color of the bear but added huge arms with claws. When it was time for Back to School Night, the bulletin board displayed the children's work of every bear looking the same—just like the teacher's model of it—except her sons. He wasn't afraid to show his creativity and demand that his vision stay true. Only 1 out of 25 came forward with enough confidence and pride in their making.

That was 20 years ago. I'm sure there are lots of bulletin boards within school buildings that display children's work that all look the same. The truth is that we are not all the same, we are very different in so many beautiful and wonderful ways.

Are we forcing each other to give up our creativity and imagination because someone decides it is the right way to do this? Is someone else's creation the one in which we strive to copy? Are we being led to believe that our creativity is not valued? If we take away all judgement and appreciate the uniqueness in others, would the results be different in the classroom and in life? I believe it would be.

Family Nights and Learning Together

Sometimes the unexpected gives us a chance to find something even greater than we could have planned. During our Family Fitness Night at school, all of the sessions were in place. We planned it out perfectly. The gym teachers gathered, planned and set up the gym to be used for fitness stations all adorned with jump ropes, obstacle courses, and gymnastic mats where students could tumble. Tables outside the gym held blood pressure screenings for parents and information packets on reducing stress and healthy eating.

In the cafeteria, the head of Food Services offered to demonstrate and involve parents and kids in cooking up some zucchini and squash. All the parents were excited to learn that their children would attend a Kids Yoga session. The parents gathered in the space and the students selected a mat and excitedly started stretching. After a while we noticed the instructor did not show up. Parents were whispering and staff was getting uneasy to think that this special moment was going to be ruined. One of the parents asked if she could help the kids begin a movement. Other parents offered to show a different pose. One at a time each parent contributed to sharing in the fun. It went from a Pinterest Perfect set-up to a real-life, problem solving precious moment. The children loved working out with their parents. The tree pose created laughter of imbalance and then concentration. The downward dog provided an imaginary thought of mountains and each parent added their little imaginary flair to explaining it to their child and the group. Parents were for a small moment, children themselves and loved every minute.

We still have our Family Fitness Nights and parents and kids are happy to be together, spending quality time. These family nights provide a break from the stresses of life and fill everyone's soul and spirit with a renewed energy and enthusiasm and love of life.

It takes great courage and confidence to believe in yourself and trust in your ideas and intuition. You can achieve a sense of calmness, not anxiety, because you are comfortable and confident with your work. You don't need the approval of others. They are your ideas and creativity. Stand proud and be who you were meant to be. Celebrate that in yourself and your children.

Parents at the art show I discussed earlier, were worried about what others might say or wanting others to praise how beautiful the picket fence came out. They feared their own ideas or artwork wouldn't have been enough. We are enough! We have been made to share our talents and light with the world.

Social media creates a false sense of reality when posts are carefully planned and executed to exhibit the "perfect" situation, emotion, etc. Pinterest hosts an array of ideas and designs but paralyze our reliance on our intuition and creativity. Adults as well as kids question their creative brain and, for fear of judgement of others or expectations of perfection, do not jump into a creative exploration at school and/or at home.

Because of this tug of war with reality and a perception of being "perfect", schools and communities are including Social Emotional Learning into the school day. Opportunities for students to discuss issues related to Self-Awareness, Self-Management, Social-Awareness, Relationship Skills, and Responsible Decision-Making. Mindfulness magazines and books fill the shelves of grocery stores and bookshops.

CASEL (The Collaborative for Social Emotional Learning) in 2013 set up a way to understand these 5 Core Competencies. They have been working for over 20 years to help create learning environments where all students can thrive. The chart at the end of this chapter will hopefully help yourself and your students and/or children at home, school, and in life. It can help you work through some difficult situations. If you see that you or your child are having difficulty feeling confident or seemed stressed, you can help them by offering up some discussion starters. Always reach out to school guidance counselors and doctors for advice as well if you're concerned with any of these Core Competencies.

Self-Awareness

Self-awareness takes time as it is the moment we start to be reflective in our own emotions, thoughts, and values. It helps us to see the strengths we have when we try to learn different content and/or tasks. Think of a situation when you had to learn something new. Did you approach that learning with a sense of curiosity and allow time to learn it? Too often we put a blanket over making everyone feel good about making an effort. But it is in the "learning" that true self-awareness can take place.

Conversations with each other need to exist in an honest platform so that pieces of learning and understanding take place. It usually is the expectation to learn something quickly that gives us stress. It's okay if at first you don't succeed. Keep trying and adjusting using different strategies. You can always enlist others to help you understand, but others should not be expected to do the work for you.

Honesty will not hurt the self-esteem if there is a plan of action to achieve the goal. Without a plan then it just becomes an opinion.

Self-Management

This goes hand in hand with self-awareness because in order to regulate your emotions, thoughts, and behavior you would need to accurately recognize them first. Impulsiveness is the enemy of self-management in that it gets in the way of keeping track of your goals.

You need tremendous self-discipline and self-motivation to achieve the goal of losing weight. Turning away delicious desserts during a party is hard when you are watching your weight. The same would apply for attending to learning something new.

When my older son was diagnosed with ADD it was difficult for me to understand why he couldn't organize himself. He would forget to do his homework and he always forgot some notebook or textbook that was needed for that assignment. I would drop everything and run back to the school to help him get what he needed. Once we realized his limitations, we set out to make his life and our lives easier. We decided to color code his subjects. This allowed him to quickly pick up what he needed out of his locker when changing classes in middle school and high school. His folder, binder, notebook, and book-sock covering for his textbook always matched. Grab and go was our way of helping him self-manage himself at school. One goal at a time.

Social-Awareness

It takes a tremendous amount of respect and empathy to understand the lives of others. It is not a simple formula that if you were born under certain circumstances that your life will be positive or negative. Situations happen that change the course of the path you take in life. Let's begin with respect. Respect is feeling a sense of work or value that you attach to yourself or others. When you look at others do you judge them on how they treat you and others? Are they honest? Do they consistently do good things? Respect starts with yourself.

What is needed to have self-respect?

◊   Being honest with yourself and others.

◊   Valuing academics and other forms of education.

◊   Taking care of your mind and body with proper nutrition and exercise.

◊   Learning to listen and understand the beliefs of others.

◊   Having responsibility of your actions.

◊   Knowing when and how to apologize.

◊   Obtaining and Managing Goals (Personal and Academic).

Once you have respect for yourself and others you can start to have empathy for those around you that are struggling socially. What ways can we help others feel welcome or heard? Empathy is not feeling sorry for someone, having pity and then giving them something just to cheer them up. Empathy requires us to just put ourselves into someone else's shoes, and try to understand what others are going through deeply.

Relationship Skills

Building our relationship skills can help us understand who we are so we can trust our intuition and creativity. It isn't easy to communicate with others if we are not sure of who we are as human beings. We help students in school identify their role when working in groups. We assign jobs, and they carry out their role to work toward a common goal or task that is set out by the teacher.

There are times more often than not that the group has a difference of opinion and some members have a set way of doing things that they want others to follow. This requires all members to come to the table to communicate, listen and cooperate with each other. There are, however, times when students give up their ideas, creativity and voice. The peer-pressure might inhibit a person from being their true self. If one takes a passive role in relationship skills because they don't have conflict-resolution skills, it will spin them into a world of unresolved issues.

Responsible Decision-Making

Each day we have opportunities to make decisions that affect our environment. Whether it's deciding to save the planet by keeping the earth clean or thinking about sustainability in our neighborhoods and towns, our decisions are important. So many times during the school day students interact with each other and we certainly promote positive behavior.

Words hold so much power because they can heal or hurt others. As we discuss perfection or the lack of it throughout this chapter it is important to remember that we are responsible for our actions. I'm sure many of your parents, as well as mine, reminded you, "actions speak louder than words."

Questions to open discussions with your <u>child/student:</u>	**Self-Awareness** The ability to	**Self-Management** The ability to
◊ What are you good at in school/ home? How do you know you're good at it? ◊ When learning a concept is hard, what do you do to help yourself? ◊ When you're stressed, what can you do to help yourself achieve your goal or help yourself?	accurately recognize one's own emotions, thoughts, and values and how they influence behavior. The ability to accurately assess one's strengths and limitations, with a well-grounded sense of confidence, optimism, and a "growth mindset." ◊ Identifying emotions ◊ Accurate self-perception ◊ Recognizing strengths ◊ Self-confidence ◊ Self-efficacy	successfully regulate one's emotions, thoughts, and behaviors in different situations—effectively managing stress, controlling impulses, and motivating oneself. The ability to set and work toward personal and academic goals. ◊ Impulse control ◊ Stress management ◊ Self-discipline ◊ Self-motivation ◊ Goal-setting ◊ Organizational skills

	Social-Awareness	Relationship Skills
◊ How can we help others feel welcome in our house and school building? ◊ What can you do to help others hear what you are saying or understand your ideas etc.?	**The ability to** take the perspective of and empathize with others, including those from diverse backgrounds and cultures. The ability to understand the social and ethical norms for behavior and to recognize family, school, and community resources and supports. ◊ Perspective-taking ◊ Empathy ◊ Appreciating diversity ◊ Respect for others	The ability to establish and maintain healthy and rewarding relationships with diverse individuals and groups. The ability to communicate clearly, listen well, cooperate with others, resist inappropriate social pressure, negotiate conflict constructively, and seek and offer help when needed. ◊ Communication ◊ Social engagement ◊ Relationship-building ◊ Teamwork

◊ When you're working with others, what helps you decide what to say or do?	<u>Responsible Decision-Making</u> The ability to make constructive choices about personal behavior and social interactions based on ethical standards, safety concerns, and social norms. The realistic evaluation of consequences of various actions, and a consideration of the well-being of oneself and others. ◊ Identifying problems ◊ Analyzing situations ◊ Solving problems ◊ Evaluating ◊ Reflecting ◊ Ethical responsibility

Developing these core competencies can lead to a healthy and productive life free from the fear of not being perfect. By using this information provided by CASEL we can begin having important conversations with our students and children. Spending time and being present can make all the difference. Can you find ways to listen when your student or child is having difficulty in any of these areas?

Reflect on some ways we are contributing to giving our students and children the wrong messages. Do we do the assignments for them? Give them the answers before they can work through the problem? Do they wait and become silent enough that we step in and "fix" it for them? So many school assignments have been overtaken by parents who do the project for their kids hoping that the "perfect" display will yield a high grade. What emotional message is the child receiving by this act? Is this act making them crippled to move ahead in their thinking and creating?

For everyone who has a presence around children, reflect on these competencies and suggestions above. Children know when you are genuine by hearing the tone of your voice and seeing your body language. Patience, respect and empathy are all part of understanding how to help out the disengaged and troubled kids today.

"When a flower doesn't bloom, you fix the environment in which it grows, not the flower."
~ Alex Den Heijer

Children are who they are. They have the capability of greatness and come to us with beautiful and unique talents. Fill out the survey to find out where your area of intelligence falls.

We are all smart in different ways. Check the box(es) that match your unique self.

Visual/Spatial Intelligence	Logical/Mathematical Intelligence
☐ I like to draw and doodle.	
☐ I like color and interesting designs.	☐ I like to solve math problems.
☐ I like books, pictures, maps, and charts.	☐ I like math and using computers.
☐ I close my eyes and see clear pictures.	☐ I reason things out.
☐ I like videos, movies and photographs.	☐ I like strategy games.
	☐ I like to use numbers to measure and analyze.
Verbal/Linguistic Intelligence	**Bodily/Kinesthetic Intelligence**
☐ I like to write.	☐ I like to use my hands to make things.
☐ I like to read books and magazines.	☐ I can't sit too long.
☐ I like to tell jokes and/or stories.	☐ I use my hands when speaking.
☐ I quote things I've read.	☐ I learn by doing rather than by watching.
☐ I listen to the radio, TV and download tunes.	☐ I touch things to learn more about them.
Naturalist	**Musical/Rhythmic Intelligence**
☐ I like to spend time outside in nature.	☐ I can remember songs.
☐ I observe the details of plants, flowers and animals.	☐ I listen to music when I study.
☐ I like to take care of plants and animals.	☐ I tap and keep the rhythm.
☐ I can hear animal and bird sounds clearly.	☐ I enjoy singing.
☐ I know the names of plants and animals.	☐ I like to listen to music.

Interpersonal Intelligence	Intrapersonal Intelligence
☐ I like working in groups.	☐ I like to work alone.
☐ I have lots of friends.	☐ I have confidence in myself.
☐ I am comfortable in a crowd.	☐ I enjoy making by myself.
☐ I have empathy for others.	☐ I know about my feelings, strengths and weaknesses.
☐ People seek my advice.	☐ I think about things and I plan what to do next.

Which box has the most checks? Sometimes there is a close second. Review all the checks and have a deep conversation of how you learn now and in the past.

Being Present Not Perfect at School

Students throughout the day are engaged in rigorous and challenging work. They are placed under pressure to move through lessons and instruction that will help them develop academically and emotionally. In all of this, creativity needs to be present. Giving our students a chance to infuse the arts into some of those lessons will create a feeling of excitement and help them take risks. Creativity takes courage. Courage to think differently and solve problems. Courage to work through the task at hand knowing the outcome might be incorrect. Learning takes time and it cannot be expected to be perfect from the start. The joy comes in savoring the moments while we are present in it. If at the time of learning students experience difficulty, they must be reminded by the adults and their peers that it's okay to make mistakes. Mistakes help inform us, reveal things we didn't at first, and slow us down a bit to make us reflect and process the changes needed to make it better. We need to help our students see that perfection is not the goal in education. Education is meant to help us attain the knowledge needed to make the world a better place. To live a long, full and happy life.

Being Present at Home

Children will go through many stages of development. The conversations and actions of those around them will impact their view of themselves and others. Whether you are together doing chores around the house or playing a pick-up game in the backyard, the words used to surround the activity is one of kindness and understanding. The patience to see that children will need time to figure it out and practice before they are expected to be independent people in the world. Small steps toward a bigger goal, small steps in learning the basics, and building upon that learning to deepen their understanding. If we find the time to be together as a family, it must be a safe place to offer ideas and try them out without placing a label or opinion. Always encourage and use words of acceptance rather than comparing their thoughts, actions or words to siblings, friends and/or family.

CREATIVE CUES

Beauty in the Imperfection

Create an opportunity to discuss the imperfect and its beauty. What makes the Leaning Tower of Pisa so beautiful? Why do broken pieces of tiles that make the most beautiful mosaics? Find items around you and your community that show how imperfections can be beautiful.

Stop and Notice

Find a moment to stop and make others aware that we will agree to be present in this moment and listen to each other. Notice the time and place and surroundings that make you focus in on the details of that moment.

Be Still

Have the patience to let the process of learning or understanding happen. Breathe and stay calm in knowing that the beauty of creativity will reveal itself. Slow down just a bit to notice the details, and be okay with the steps that might have to happen to let the truth and creativity come to life.

Attitude of Gratitude

We can easily be aware around the month of November when everyone is focused on having gratitude in what we have done or need to do to achieve the goal we set forth for ourselves. But truthfully, anytime is a perfect time for carving out space to become mindful of all the blessings we have in our lives. Lots of journaling and drawing pictures. Sharing those thoughts and visual images is a great way to connect ourselves and show them you are present in their lives.

CREATIVITY BREAK

Design a music album cover

Imagine if you could listen to the music and design a new cover for your favorite artist. Listen and move your pen, marker, pencil to where it feels the sounds, rhythms, and patterns. Add in details using crayons, paints, colored markers, etc.

KEY #3

SET UP YOUR SPACE

It Matters

"All space is space in which to create."
~ Eric Maisel

My 6th grade art teacher was tall and very skinny. Her curly hair had streaks of natural gray making its way through. She had a flair but in a quiet sort of way. She was laid back but when it came to teaching us the elements of art she was laser focused like nobody's business.

I remember the first time she allowed us to break a crayon. Yes, break a crayon! Was she angry? Did she want us to revolt against the Crayola factory? We'd been taught to take care of our supplies and never break our pencils or anything that we brought from home or was given to us by the school.

Our teacher continued with the madness and had us tear off the paper of one of the broken pieces. She instructed us to only use the sides of crayons and not the tip. The moans and shouts of joy exploded—we saw the techniques emerging and giving light to a whole new way of thinking about our drawing.

If you put pressure on one end of the side of the crayon you can create rock surfaces and other dramatic landscape designs. So many techniques that were presented to us made our imaginations and creativity soar with how we can use these and apply these in other pieces of work.

Disappearing Crayons

"They're only crayons.
You didn't fear them in Kindergarten, why fear them now?"
~ Hugh MacLeod

Crayons! How can it be that such a small box holds so much creativity! We start off in school with a simple box of 8 or less and grow to understand the magnitude of color. To pick just the right one and test it out. To play and scribble. To place it back in its place or to search the big box looking for just the right one.

Crayons were used throughout most of my school years but slowly disappeared around 7th grade if you weren't involved with any art classes. Since art was a passion inside of me, I took as many classes as they would allow. Our supplies were more than just crayons. It expanded to pastels, chalk, markers, fine point markers to outline our drawings, small pallets of paint, and brushes.

We learned to wet the paper first instead of applying color to the brush. We dipped our plastic flimsy brushes into the water and smothered the paper and then the magic began. More paint on the brush meant deeper colors and bleeding effects. We watched in amazement as the drops of color spread all over the paper. The farther away it went from the point of dropping the lighter the effect. Toothbrushes were used. Just like brushing your teeth, we brushed the hard square paint and happily flicked the bristles and again we created more techniques.

Art class was a place I could lose myself to my creative mind. My imagination grew as I thought about splashes of waves against the rocks and clouds in the sky that could be these beautiful pink and orange bursts of bleeding on my paper.

I remember the day my art teacher asked us to bring in a ruler. We were all confused. Math in art? What kind of measuring would we do in art? What was this all about? We ran to class as if beating the bell and the rest of our classmates would give us the right to be privy to finding out. Middle school perspective drawing was the focus. We used our rulers to draw diagonal lines that reached a point on the horizon. Everything drawn on that line had to follow the angle of the line. Geometry and art became infused. Vocabulary words were used to describe our drawings. Parallel, perpendicular, rays all became common language and new to all of us. We made buildings, lamp posts, fences, all going in the same direction toward the point on the horizon.

Our desks were our creative space—our castle and our home of happiness during the school day. Art class not only gave way to our creative minds, but filled our intellectual brains with vocabulary we wouldn't have gotten until 10th grade Geometry.

Art Class Lessons

When I think back to my art teacher making us break our crayons, I think she knew she was helping us find our creative space within our work. The physical shape of the crayon didn't matter, what mattered was our approach to having an open mind, a creative mindset of the many possibilities of that broken crayon. I remember she wanted us to bring in a shoebox. All of our art supplies had to be in a shoebox. It was pure genius. Did it matter if we had a fancy table, a chair, or a corner to go too? Of course not! What mattered was wherever our supplies could be found we were one with them. We opened the lid of our shoeboxes and each time seemed different. It looked different or maybe as we grew to understand what each pencil, crayon, marker (fine point and chisel) could do to our lines, shapes, designs, pure magic would happen. The space of our supply box created the space and time to be creative. To unlock the creative child because we had in front of us the limitless possibilities of hope, change, and inspiration.

Taking Art Class Home – My First Creative Space

How I longed to continue what I learned in class at home ... to become part of my home life. I would race home and tell my parents everything I learned in art. Sharing my pictures and artwork became commonplace. They knew I needed a space to call my own for this creative journey.

In my childhood home, my family lived upstairs and my grandparents lived in a small apartment downstairs. The upstairs consisted of three bedrooms, a small bathroom, kitchen and a living room and dining room all on the same floor. If I visited my grandparents, their space was even smaller. There were no elaborate tables or fancy desks with organizational features. There was however a basement that my father decided to finish in the 70's with dark brown paneling and indoor/outdoor carpeting. The basement was used to hold family parties and get togethers as well as a space to do laundry. As you walked down the stairs of this basement, there was a large area to the right of the stairs that led to a door. The door led to the backyard. We played ping pong, darts, and hide-and-seek in the space off to the right. But off to the left of the stairs was a room with no windows. There were two closets, used to hold winter coats and games as well as old photos and memorabilia.

By high school, I was heavily into drawing and painting and I saw that small space to the left a perfect spot for me to create. Mom and Dad placed a small folding table and a desk light inside. It was there that I would spend many hours creating. I hung posters from a magazine called "Art & Man." It was like the Scholastic Newspaper in the schools of today, only it was better quality paper and it always had the most beautiful photographs of artwork around the classrooms. We could find art history articles and beautiful pictures of famous pieces of art. Without knowing, I was creating my own vision board. Walls were filled with artwork, art history, and even my own work taped to the brown paneling.

All of the worries and peer pressure situations were dissolved when I entered that space. I felt like I was floating on air and time stood still. I would work down there for hours creating, making, drawing, painting, and sewing just to name a few. There wasn't anything I couldn't do or dream about. That space was a remedy for my awkward teenage years and it was there that I would hone my artistic skills.

When I think of today's conveniences of organizational systems, dollar store plastic storage baskets, and fancy desk chairs, I'm amused to think what I would've been able to do. There were no fancy organization systems in my time. All my supplies were in shoeboxes. Old cookie tins were used for broken crayons and pastels. Coffee cans held my brushes and pencils and pens. Masking tape held posters, pictures, and artwork on the brown paneled walls. Folding chairs were perfect shelves for my shoe boxes. If I needed my singer sewing machine, I took it out of the white case and placed it on the folding table. If I pressed the pedal of the sewing machine too hard the whole table shook and immediately I slowed down. If I was really adventurous I'd sneak upstairs into my grandmother's 1936 Singer sewing machine that was set inside a beautiful commode with drawers on each side. It didn't have fancy stitches or backstitching button but it made the most beautiful straight stitch I've ever seen to this day.

That space in the basement became a go-to place when I needed to fill my spirit with joy. I could come upstairs out of the darkness and be able to face the challenges of childhood and puberty because I was immersed in the making each day. The space—the quiet uninterrupted space allowed me to test out my learning and curiosity to see what creations I could make. I remember taking my old jeans (dungarees we called them back in the 70s) and looking at the back pockets as an opportunity to make a purse. I used my embroidery floss to write messages and symbols of happiness. My grandmother even taught me to put a snap onto it.

Once I was given a set of colored pencils—a set of 40. I couldn't believe that when I added water to the paper they melted into a dreamy state of rainbow clouds. There were two closets, one was under the steps and the other was a cedar closet where my mom placed all of our winter coats and her fancy dresses from past weddings she attended with my dad. At the bottom of the closet my mother kept our work, projects and artwork from our past school years. The room wasn't big but it was pure heaven to me. There was a lamp that had a bendable neck and I would move it constantly to try to get enough light especially when I was sketching. On the table I kept all my pencils in recycled tomato cans and glass jars to hold my water and another one for my brushes. Shoeboxes (which I learned from my art teacher) was a perfect place to put all my paper cuttings, glue, scissors, pencils. One was for paints and others just held random folded paper and even cut up stencils. Funny how I didn't think about shelving or swivel chairs or fancy decorations. I had my space, my get away spot to lose myself to my imagination and ideas.

When I wanted to sew I would either go upstairs to my grandmother's apartment or stay downstairs in the basement and deal with the machine and the wobbly folding table shaking if the pressed the pedal too hard. I had cut-up the legs of the jeans to make small cross-body bags or little pouches to keep my thread and needles—I added buttons and snaps too. It truly didn't matter what I did or what the room looked like I was involved in the "making."

Home economics was not wasted on me. I loved all the sewing projects because I could share those experiences with my family and practice my skills in a space all my own. My brother and sister didn't bother me. They loved to play outside for hours. I rode my bike and played outside too but there was something special about that space in my basement.

Setting up Your Space At Home

Our homes can be a place of rest, exploration and creativity. Finding that special spot can be challenging but it doesn't have to be separate for you and your children. We as parents can show our children how easy it is to settle into a creative moment by modeling that for them. What space do you use to find that special time to draw, paint, knit, build, etc.? Do we allow our children to see us involved in some quiet creative time?

You don't need a basement or separate room. My sons didn't have a basement to call their own. The small eat-in kitchen became their space. Now I took advantage of those modern organizational systems, yes, I brought those plastic stackable bins. I bought some plastic stackable bins to hold their building supplies like Legos and blocks. I would find lots of sales on crayons, markers, scissors, glue and any and all office supplies, especially around August and September when school supply shopping was on everyone's minds.

The loose-leaf paper reinforcers became sticky eyes on their drawings. Old newspapers were stacked in case they painted and I needed to cover the table. Construction paper pieces were in a bin because you never knew what color you'd need. Paper was cut, curled around a pencil, torn, ripped and frayed. Experimenting all the ways paper can change its form was magical to my boys. They would take over my dining room space to build with Legos and K'Nex. Who uses a dining room anyway? Spaces like these only seem important around the holidays when family and friends would gather. Valuable space that goes untouched becomes a perfect spot.

If you haven't found that special place for yourself then it's the perfect time to make it a family project. Parents and children can set up a spot and ask all family members what they want that special place to have. Helping them see that it might be important to have proper lighting, storage, and furniture that everyone can take part in. You can even put some personal touches to help your child feel comfortable creating there.

Space can be found anywhere in a house. The space doesn't have to be enormous. Utilizing corners seems perfect for gathering and creating. Spaces at home can consist of converting a kitchen table or dining room table into a creative space. Can a snack table suffice? Sure as it depends on the size of the project. You can create just sitting on a chair, couch or picnic table. Your backyard is a wide open space that lends itself to curiosity and imagination. Lay down a sheet, quilt or blanket and the backyard can become a way to take in the outside.

Where do we house all the supplies needed to be creative?

Today many parents shop in the Dollar Store for organizational items to house all the creative supplies needed, but recycled coffee cans, shoeboxes and take out containers work just as well. Compartments and organizers can be found even on the back of your car seat. I found this really cool plastic lap desk for a small amount of money. There were two plastic compartments; one on each side that could house crayons, pencils, markers and scissors, glue safely. It reminded me of a "breakfast-in-bed tray," but it could work in the back-seat of a car, any space in a house and, of course, a classroom. Sometimes I think a tackle-box can work just as well. You can carry it around in the house, in the car, and even take it on vacation. All your supplies in one spot. Of course you might need a larger tote bag if you're in need of paper, canvas, cardboard, etc. Even under your child's bed can be a perfect space to fit supplies in shoeboxes.

Here's a dual purpose list of ideas for things you probably have in your home already:

◊ Cookie Tins with lids: cut-up paper, fabric scraps, glue sticks

◊ Coffee Cans - pencils, paintbrushes, toothbrushes, markers

◊ Plastic Take-Out Containers: buttons, felts pieces, pom-poms

◊ Shoeboxes: crayons, markers, brushes, paint sets, pastel kits, erasers, fabric

◊ Mason Jars: use on their side and hot glue to make a wide organizational system for separating crayons, markers, brushes, pencils, popsicle sticks

◊ Breakfast-in-Bed Tray: portable desk

◊ Cookie Sheets: magnetic letters, paint palette, finger painting surface

Setting up Your Space at School

At school a child's desk or their locker can be their creative spot. Some students decorate their lockers and have supplies in their to grab in between classes. Some students can sit outside their classrooms by their lockers and have their creative space be mobile. It doesn't have to be a set location it can change throughout the year. I've seen corners or classrooms with bean-bags and beach chairs as a place where creativity can come alive.

If your child knows the importance of finding a creative space they can create anywhere they go. This mindset allows them an open mind to decide, "I'm here. I'm in my space." All of sudden the child forgets where he is and what time it is because he is so involved in the creative process. The space allows our children to be free and distraction free to let their creative minds open to the art of "making."

Schools have always had creativity existing in art classes around the country. Students knew they could have a time in their week to dive in and use their creativity and imagination during art.

Misconceptions in our society keep pulling us away from creativity. They would have us believe that it's just for the artistic souls. But throughout the years there have been "makers." Our human nature lends itself to design and create things with our hands and tools.

Infusing Creativity in Science, Technology, and Math

In 2013, the American Libraries Magazine published a short, *History of Making*, timeline. Even as far back as the early 1900 libraries played a role in providing a makerspace for quilting, sewing and knitting. Libraries have always been a space to not only collect information but to share ideas through collaboration and creativity.

When MIT's FAB LAB gained popularity, it brought

about an awareness of digital tools that could enhance "making".

"Fab Labs, are designed to fabricate things,
and consist of digital equipment for designing products
and the digitally driven tools to create them."
~ Burke

In 2009, President Obama created even more interest when he launched the "Educate to Innovate" campaign. He wanted the leaders of the educational world to value "making."

"I want us all to think about new and creative ways
to engage young people in science and engineering,
whether it's science festivals, robotics competitions, fairs
that encourage young people to create and build and invent—to
be makers of things, not just consumers of things."
~ Barack Obama

Today museums, schools, and libraries have committed themselves to integrate makerspaces as part of their curriculum through the library/media classes. These are rooms set aside or as part of an existing space dedicated for children to design, tinker, construct, and test their imaginations and inventions. Science, Technology, Engineering, Art, and Mathematics (S.T.E.A.M) are now part of a curriculum for children. Here they are exposed to creating, coding, building, inventing, and of course, art is infused into all of it.

Makerspaces house all kinds of art and building materials such as sticks, toothpicks, marshmallows, cardboard, pom poms, etc. According to Ann Taylor, "We have come to think of educational architecture as a 'three-dimensional textbook,' a learning environment that is a functional art form, a place of beauty, and a motivational center for learning."

Desks are now replaced with a wide open space that contain moveable desks that interlock for working in groups or individually. Cabinets and shelves house all kinds of re-cyclable materials to use for "making." Technology such as Chromebook, iPads, 3-D printers and programming equipment has a home in these spaces as well.

My school district, under the leadership of Dr. Marc Natanagara, Assistant Superintendent and Supervisor of Technology, Tiffany Lucey, has brought Makerspace in full force from 2014 until present. Working in collaboration with the Jay and Linda Grunin Foundation we were able to renovate all 17 school buildings with a makerspace focus. Additionally Dr. Natanagara and Tiffany Lucey hold a state-wide JS MakerFest which is a free, non-profit annual community event. This event consists of around 100 maker booths and workshops, a drone/RC field, EDTalks, competitive and instructional robotics arenas and a Green Fair too. Over the past four years there have been over 400 makers and 14,000 attendees joining in the fun.

On a school wide effort, my elementary school, for the

past three years has celebrated "makers" by holding a *Parent Academy* event called S.T.E.A.M Night. We hold this event in our large gymnasium where one side of the gym is sectioned off to allow the High School Robotics club to show our elementary students how they can use S.T.E.A.M to build and program robots.

In the space where the High School students proudly displayed their learning were opportunities for our students to try out simple coding and programing using Webots(™), Bebots(™), Ozobots(™) and Sphero's(™). All of these devices utilize an iPad app that helps students to practice coding which is a simple word for programming the object to move or change color. Children program the device to follow a path or code it to move in different ways and even to change color. The students were amazed to see that technology isn't just about playing a video game and earning points and rewards. Students had a chance to practice their creativity and imagination through technology.

On the other half of the gym are S.T.E.A.M activities but using everyday items to solve a problem. We wanted to challenge students to see if they could design, test and solve problems at hand using everyday objects like popsicle sticks, rubber bands, paper, glue, magnets, cups, etc. We had spaces filled with opportunities for students to build. Home Depot collaborates each year in providing students with wood and building tools. Our students have made bird houses, toolboxes, and an easel.

Can you make a bag to carry your things using duct tape?

This table has lots of "makers" visiting. One year a mom and her daughter decided to design and create cross-body bags.

Can you build a tower with plastic cups? Students are always motivated to compete with one another in this area to see who can build the highest tower. This challenge causes students to think about structure and load. Architects and engineers in the making.

What if we took caps from our bottles of various colors and sizes, could we make a mural? We did just that. For several months before this event, families and children were encouraged to collect their bottle caps from school lunches and/or home and bring them into a large bin located in the main lobby. Children were excited to see the amount growing each day and wondered what it will be used for.

When S.T.E.A.M night came around they saw a huge piece of plywood and bins of caps sorted by color. Several bottles of wood glue was provided and away they went. With no instructions necessary these students created a beautiful mural of trees, birds, and nature which now hangs in our library/makerspace for all to enjoy. Children of all ages were excited to visit each station including this bottle cap mural.

Although each station had a problem or challenge, and students needed to think constructively and creatively to solve it, there was always a different approach used by the children that would show that their approach and outcomes will always be unique and different—just like them. Like all of us, we need to celebrate our uniqueness and not be afraid to trust our intuition and imagination.

Making the Vision Come to Life

You're probably wondering how did we fund this effort and make it happen? With the generosity of the Jay and Linda Grunin Foundation providing $10,000 to each school, as mentioned above, we knew we needed more to make this space happen. In 2015 our school decided to create a renovation committee that would address the outdated areas of the school. The library was outdated and we had this beautiful space in the back of the school that needed a little TLC. We all worked together to raise money, write grants and commit ourselves to providing these creative learning spaces for our students. The library was our number one priority. Our librarian wrote a grant and was awarded $10,000 from Ocean First Bank. We fundraised $17,000 more. This included cupcake and pretzel sales, candy-grams, and a read-a-thon.

This school wide effort was made clear to parents and students and they read as many books as they could during the winter and spring. In this model classroom that would include a makerspace, we gathered our ideas for providing a space that would encourage learning. Space that could become new learning environments. Our committee worked together to brainstorm a space that would inspire curiosity, critical thinking and the freedom of thought. The committee also worked together with high school design students to draw up the architectural plans and work together with us. The district changed the lighting, ripped up the old carpet and installed new flooring as well as a fresh coat of paint.

Our fund-raising efforts allowed us to purchase an indoor growing lab. This lab would connect with the curriculum and students would be able to study plants in the winter. We devoted one half of the library to house all our makerspace items for our S.T.E.A.M night.

Creative spaces weren't only built for the inside of this library. Outside, we worked together with the Eagle Scouts and the school district groundskeepers to design growing beds with gates and wires to keep out animals that would destroy our gardens. Picnic tables were rearranged to provide small group learning. Benches were provided so that children can observe plant life and the ecosystem that engulfed this outdoor learning area. Here in this space students can see the relationship between animals, plants and the environment. Children as young as 6 years old can learn about the structure of a plant, the life-cycle of a plant, and how that goes together with weather and climate in this outdoor space.

When we free our minds and allow curiosity and questioning to drive our learning, there is no limit to what we can do. It is clear that we need all children, parents and community members to work together to have an interest and responsibility in children's education.

Making space can happen from a corner of your home to an entire 10,000 square foot school building. Here are some creative cues that will help you remember what we discussed in this chapter.

CREATIVE CUES

Designing your home space can be a little challenging if you're living in a small apartment or home. But don't worry as we discussed above there are many opportunities to create portable creative spaces. If you have some space set aside here are some ideas:

Cabinent Comfort

You can easily find an old piece of furniture or repurpose a chest or hutch and create a space to relax. Garage sales and even Facebook marketplace have items people are happy to donate and give away for a small amount of money. Look for cabinets that have enough space to keep all your supplies organized at the same time. You can create a precious moment by painting it together with your children.

Garden Grandeur

Gardens have a way of pulling us into their world. Creating a space outside by the trees can invoke creativity. If you have a room that overlooks a garden or trees that would be perfect on winter days where you can let the outside come into your home.

Peace and Quiet

We all need peace and quiet especially after our lives are moving at such a fast pace and we overschedule ourselves. Find a creative space that's away from distractions such as televisions, computers and high traffic areas such as the kitchen. Comfortable seating and desk space can help children become actively involved and develop the skills they need to navigate through life now and in the future.

Encourage S.T.E.A.M in Your Children's School

If your school does not have a Makerspace, create a committee that shares this vision and get to work. First, organize a meeting with your administration and start to plan out where funds could be used to renovate and update. As everyone's needs differ it will depend on how much or how little you need done regarding construction.

Fundraising efforts take a lot of work from the school and committee members to work together and begin the campaign. Remember to enlist the help of community organizations and businesses that will join you in this effort. They need you and the parents of your school as much as you need them. It takes more than a village . . . but it can be done.

Start checking out some makerspaces online and create a list of items that will need to be purchased. Sometimes attaching an item to a business or organization will make your fundraising easier. Reach out to the American Legions and other non-profits in your area to see if they would be able to fund these specific items.

While you're waiting for the space to be completed with construction and supplies, hold a small Makerspace event and invite parents to test out some creative challenges to see the impact of this innovative way to learn.

When the space is complete and all supplies are ready to go, celebrate with a ribbon cutting event and invite groups to tour your new creative space.

What if you already have a Makerspace? No worries, let's just check in to see if you are making the best of it. The supplies below will help!

Everyday Supplies:

*Scissors, rulers, pencils, crayons, markers (*Need large supply of these 5 items)

Tape: all different kinds (duct tape, scotch tape, masking tape)

Empty toilet paper and paper towel rolls

Cardboard: all shapes and sizes

Blocks /Legos

Fabric

Recycled containers: all sizes and shapes

Straws

Pipe cleaners

Balloons

Play-Doh

LEDs: Light Emitting Diodes for experiments

Batteries (CR2032)

Copper foil tape

Robotic, Coding and 3D machines:

Makey Makey: turn bananas and other fruit into touch-pads

Sphero: Robotic ball controlled by an app

Snap Circuits (used to build AM radios, alarms, door-bells, etc.

K'Nex

Lego: WeDo 2.0, S.T.E.A.M Park, Simple Machines, Mindstors EV3

Ozobots: coding

3Doodler: draw in the air designing 3D objects with a Pen

CREATIVITY BREAK

Find a few crayons. Peel back the wrapper and break the crayons—size and shape doesn't matter. Just have fun on a piece of scrap paper or even draw here on this page. Begin experimenting with the way the broken crayon colors and shades. Flip the crayon on one side or the other, tilt it slightly, scrape the color onto the page. There are no rules. If you want to get really crazy, glue the crayons to a canvas. Place a blow-dryer over the top at high heat and watch the colors melt and make accidental art.

KEY #4

EMBRACE MESSY

Learning Always Is

"Tell me and I forget,
Teach me and I remember,
Involve me and I learn."
~Benjamin Franklin

In 2006 I was given grant money to study Lighthouses in my classroom (Lighthouses and Literacy). My third graders were immersed not only studying the local lighthouses in the areas but given the chance to create lighthouses of the future. The messiness of their learning came in spending months diving into books, literature and field trips that would help them gather understanding of why lighthouses existed, how they worked and the beautiful and varied structures that made them all different. We decided as a class to make a documentary film about The Twin Lights. They broke into groups and divided out the various parts of what they wanted to create for this film.

During their lunch and recess time, they were writing, creating, rehearsing, reworking and changing what they wanted to say to have it ready for the day of our filming. Day after day, they worked together, some easier than others, but all the while knowing that the day of filming they had to be ready. On the day of the field trip, each group gathered outside the lighthouse and with the help of parent volunteers, each group picked a location and got right into the filming. It was all business. Third graders—filmmakers—using a small flip-camera purchased with the grant money, got right to work. They collaborated, some argued about where they wanted the camera to be, but through the messiness of working and reworking their parts, they communicated their facts using props, background scenery, and parts of the lighthouse museum. Their learning wasn't a clear path, it was made up of many months of providing an encouraging environment and a safe place to open their minds to what could be. They were allowed to be creative and think of possibilities. To take their newly learned knowledge and apply it in a new way.

Creating Without Fear of Judgment

In the 70s you weren't worried about social media and "Perfectly Pinterest"—you were just you. I was just a young girl, surrounded by strong and confident women at home and even on TV. I wanted to be Rhoda on the Mary Tyler Moore Show. Rhoda was independent and charismatic, not to mention she had a hot lover . . . Joe. Her flair and creativity spoke to me. Not that Mary Tyler Moore didn't, but my mom and sister were more like her—always doing the right thing and never getting into trouble.

I was the messy one—the one that didn't fuss over her hair or clothes. The one that dropped and broke things. The one that lost the pretty jewelry given to her for special occasions. But, I came to understand that the messiness was my innocent dive into living without fear of being judged.

Involved Learning

As Benjamin Franklin states, "Involve me and I learn." Involvement requires quite a bit of messiness. For example, to be involved in cooking a meal means that the kitchen is not going to be clean or tidy. It will be filled with pots, utensils, parts of food cut up that we will use, parts of food that's cut away because it will not be used or needed.

Learning is the same.

There should be accountable talk amongst children instead of quiet classrooms. There should be papers cut up and pencils, crayons, and markers on desks. There should be students who can sit together on the floor or at a table working with a group to figure out a concept or explaining their thinking by utilizing chart paper, construction paper or any paper. There should be technology present to assist students with furthering their knowledge in the subject area or digging deeper into a concept and reporting back their findings to the group.

Walking by classrooms that are so neat and tidy as if it popped out of a Pinterest page sends a chill through my body. Involvement is messy because perfection should not be a goal in the initial stages of learning something new.

When we think about a theory of learning that has "involvement" as its central component I think of the Constructivist Theory. This theory's central idea is that humans learn by building new knowledge upon our previous knowledge and learning is constructed. It is active learning not passive that constructs meaning. This is not something new.

As far back as 1938, John Dewey who was an American philosopher, psychologist and educational reformer stated that, "Learning is a social activity, it is something we do together, in interaction with each other, rather than an abstract concept."

So why do I witness day after day students who are disengaged? Students who can't seem to make eye contact? Students who look like they've checked out of the world around them?

Sometimes during this way of learning, we find ourselves with moments when we feel like a failure, when we can't seem to do anything right or have difficulty learning a new concept. There is something to be said about putting those broken pieces together. Finding a way to make whole the broken failed moments that can be mended, that can be whole again but in a changed way. Nothing will be the same but the learning and magical moments can come to life from the brokenness.

Remember, messiness is a temporary state. Children in the midst of creativity or learning do not see the mess. They do not see the struggle. We as adults see the mess as chaotic and uncomfortable. It is through the mess and struggle that creativity emerges.

Embracing Behavioral Messy

Two years ago I was involved in settling an unruly third grade class. Students talking to each other from across the room, getting out of their seats while the teacher was speaking and it was clear, no one was paying attention. Each day seemed to bring about another phone call to the office seeking help in classroom management and discipline. "They're the worst class I've ever had." This seemed to be the same language used year after year. Could they be that bad? I would walk upstairs to the classroom listening to the teacher's voice increase as if they would listen if she raised it even higher. "Sit down!! Where are you going? I thought I told you to get out your math book. You're not listening!"

The class was studying Harriet Tubman and the Underground Railroad. Students sat with worksheets in front of them and response questions to fill out after reading. As I approached the door I took a deep breath. The teacher quickly came to the door and threw her hands in the air, "I don't know what to do with these kids."

"I will talk to them," I said again taking a deep breath. In order to fully embrace messy, we must realize sometimes messy comes in the form of behavior as well.

My thoughts scrambled as I tried to think of something that would cure it all and be done with it, but it wasn't that simple. There are never magic words that will cure a situation because experiences need time and consistency. The words and actions need to be from a place of caring and openness. The students in class have been yelled at and I'm sure they have heard of all the ways they were not doing anything right. Negativity does not heal, love and care is the magic.

Students pick up pretty quickly how you feel about them. Your voice, your tone, and of course your body language. I knew I had to speak to them from a place of warmth and care. Instead of lecturing the class about how to behave and follow directions, I instead spoke to them questioning them about the content they were learning. We had a wonderful chat and told them about a class I had long ago who studied Harriet Tubman and made a quilt.

"A quilt?" Students questioned, "What's that?"

Some of them had never heard or seen one. The quilt was done by one of my second grade classes as a culminating project. Each student chose a quilt pattern and with fabric markers recreated the pattern. Each square represented a message.

For example, if a safe house had food, the basket quilt pattern quilt would be draped over a porch or hung outside so the runaway slaves knew they could stop there for food. They used their geometry skills to show a basket with triangles. I knew the extent my students went through to find the pattern in books and recreated it on the cloth.

It took us months as a class but the learning became real and important to them. When I spoke to the class I asked them if they wanted me to bring it in and of course, it was a resounding, "Yes!" Their curiosity for learning was evident. It was amazing how soon they forgot about their negative behavior and their minds shifted to a place of imagination and promise. Anticipation and excitement filled the room as we continued to discuss what they already learned thus far. The journey to learn more and further their knowledge took flight.

The students were so excited to see the quilt and we had so many days of visits and chats about their content and about quilts. The messages the quilts provided to the runaway slaves interested the "misbehaved" kids to the point that they said, "Can we make one?"

As I thought about how important it is for children to create, to be a maker in their journey as a student and experience the hands-on activities needed for growth, I decided to set up a Lunch and Learn program for these misbehaved kids. The kids who felt misunderstood, mismanaged and broken. I sent a note home to the whole class inviting any student to partake of sessions that would be to explore content and "sew." Yes boys were sewing each day at lunch. Mending their brokenness and bringing learning together like the fabrics they were putting together. Their hands were creating their own expression of themselves. Somewhere in those sessions, the students started to believe in themselves, to care about their making and in turn each other. Their harsh attitudes softened and this safe place became a healing place.

Small squares of solid and patterned cotton cloth were put together to make pillows. They learned how to sew a running stitch around the edges of the fabric. Amazed when we turned it inside out and stuffed it with polypill their imaginations and prior knowledge understood "Oh, that's how a pillow is made!"

Another project was to create a pouch to hold things. Some students looked at the construction of a paper envelope and recreated it with felt. They took apart the paper envelope and recognized the geometric dimensions of corners and angles when folded to create this pouch. They were excited to think about what they could fill it with. Again using running stitches to hold the corners together to make this pouch.

Because the felt was made using solid colors, I had a conversation with them about embellishment and whimsical artwork on cloth. I had books that I took out of the local library handy to show them embroidery and embellishment with clothing. Again taking the needle and thread we practiced different embroidery stitches that would help them bring life to their solid colored pouch. Beautiful embroidery floss in brilliant colors was theirs for the taking. Some of the embroidery floss I purchased but most of it was donated by the teacher whose classroom they came from. The students wailed at how wrapping thread around a needle and pushing it down into the cloth and felt could make a French knot look like pistils inside a flower or maybe antennae on an insect or alien ship. Each day they wanted to learn more and more. The fabric and yarn now were pulling their lives together. They felt confident in their making. Miraculously their behavior subsided for fear they would not get to spend time at Lunch and Learn.

During the winter months, I asked the students of Lunch and Learn to bring in an old sweater that was too small or going to be donated soon. I made them examine the sleeves of the sweater to think about what we could do to use those sleeves in a different way. To upcycle something old and worn. To give new life to the worn out and tired old sweaters that lay limp on the table. Again they had difficulty trusting their imaginations and letting their creativity out. I took one of the sleeves and placed them over my arm to cover half my hand. The bulb went off—they imagined hand warmers. Wondering questions filled . . . But where does my thumb go? How can it stay—it's too loose at the end by my elbow. Questions about design, construction, etc. The important thing to remember is that we had time. Time to wonder. Time to draw. Time to figure out the solution to the many questions they had. I let them draw and think.

Thomas Lux made us aware of our making in his poem.

"An Horatian Notion"

"You make the thing because you love the thing
And you love the thing because some else loved it

enough to make you love it.
And with that your heart like a tent peg pounded
Toward the earth's core.
And with that your heart on a beam burns
Through the ionosphere.
And with that you go to work."
~ By Poet Thomas Lux (1947 - 1917)

Passion

Love what you do, boy loving what you do can be messy. It might involve taking risks and believing in your gut instinct that tells you this feels right. Go with it. Don't be afraid of following through even if those around you don't agree. It is your pursuit of living the life you love. You can overthink it and then somehow you separate yourself from the truth that lies within. So many times I have heard people say, "But you knew you always wanted to be a teacher" or "I don't know what I'm passionate about." After high school I didn't follow the path to become a teacher because remember, as I mentioned, it was the 80's and the message was "Make Money." Advice was given to me to go for a career that makes more money than a teacher.

So off I went to secretarial school to get an associate degree and come out making more money than a teacher. I listened to society instead of myself. I landed a job on the Foreign Exchange trading floor of Goldman Sachs and it was exciting at first and full of energy. But it didn't take long for me to feel inside this wasn't what I was meant to do, so I began my journey of going back to school at night to become a teacher.

It took me years and years before I was able to call a classroom my own. It was a bittersweet experience because I loved every undergraduate and graduate class that brought me closer to my dream but at the same time I missed time with my husband, children, family and friends. Instead of being young and enjoying life, I was working full time during the day, going to school at night and spending weekends writing papers.

Passion, when you find it, runs deep within us and brings out a burning desire to see it come to life. It overtakes your life and until it is complete you don't have peace. So many people who have not tapped into what they are passionate about walk around passively not connected to the world around them and seem lifeless. There is no joy or light coming from within. Their eyes are glazed over and their body language speaks defeat. But it is never too late to find that light within! Creativity will help you reveal it.

Let us question for a moment if our environment is punishing creativity or supporting it? Are we afraid to step out and try something new? Taking a risk means you are not only outside of your comfort zone but doing something you might not have all the answers initially. When we were children we jumped into new learning experiences without our egos telling us we can't or passing judgement. If we freed ourselves from those thoughts and allowed our creative force inside come out there is no limit to what we can create and accomplish. Picasso said, "All children are artists. The problem is how to remain an artist once you grow up." Finding that inner child again can unlock your creative self. You might find your love and passion for whatever is it that you were suppressing.

In my life, I suppressed my creativity. I loved art but the message was artists can't make a living. There's no money in that career path. I grew up and entered the adult world of work and bills and responsibility. I didn't see how being creative could make money or at least I wasn't strong enough to pursue it and see where it led me. Remember, as I mentioned, it was the 80's and everything was about making money. Today it's about making meaning. When I finally made my way into teaching, I started to become confident in who I was and what I was there to do. My calling was not only to teach but to use my creativity to change the world around me and inspire the students to find their own. I made sure their learning was from a place of hands on learning. There were centers filled with every item to let creativity come alive. It's never too late.

Just because we grow up and finish out our formal schooling doesn't mean we stop learning and growing. Analyze your environment and see if children and adults are being criticized or punished for being creative. Learning . . . Active Learning should be the wings on which dreams take flight. Don't be afraid to love learning. Certainly it deserves the space and time to give to it. Just like a tree, it might take years to strengthen our roots, but our branches should reach out along different paths to gather the beautiful sunlight of learning. And yes those paths, like branches, will not be straight. They will curve and turn but will continue to grow through the rain and storms.

Curiosity

Although loving what you do is extremely important in letting our creativity come to life, there is also curiosity that plays an important role. Learning doesn't just appear because you love what you do and you can be in that learning experience for days, months and years. But curiosity helps us expand our learning and in doing so can become messy. Curiosity and wondering lead us to new territories of learning where we might find ourselves out of our comfort zone.

When my first son was born he truly was curious about everything around him. He wanted to know. "Mommy what's that?" I would stop and tell him the object or the thing he was pointing at whether it be outside or inside. He would gather each word and explanation like a sponge. He kept growing in his curiosity of the world. At four years old he couldn't get enough of dinosaurs, he wanted to know every name for them and he saw the differences and observed the body structure. I tried to find plastic replicas of them at learning stores. I purchased books with pictures and details, puzzles to put the T-Rex together. As parents, we try to support our children's curiosity. It was funny how the local children's museum had a "Dinosaur" exhibit just around the time my son's curiosity was exploding.

It was amazing to see that bringing him to this exhibit truly solidified his knowledge and the experience was price-less. When we got home he couldn't wait to take out his dinosaurs and create his own exhibit with structures, dino-saurs, and people too (even if they were Lego people). As he continued to find other subjects curious like lighthouses and architectural structures, his love for dinosaurs never died out. He wanted to have his friends and family to come with him to celebrate his birthday. We all became Paleontologists that year and with paint brushes and sand we imagined discover-ing fossils of dinosaurs.

Active Learning

Active learning is needed for all children to help them grow creatively.

The first part of active learning, **Discovery**, can take place at school or at home. Finding that curiosity or love of a particular area of content.

The next part of active learning is **Processing**. Children need space and time to take the information they are learn-ing and process it.

The third part of active learning, after processing infor-mation, is to **Apply** that learning through hands-on experi-ence. When children participate in active learning they are thinking, discussing, investigating and creating.

According to Freeman, "Active Learning engages students in the process of learning through activities and/or discussions in class, as opposed to passively listening to an expert. It emphasizes higher order thinking and often involves group work."

It is natural for students to thrive in this way. Not only my son but the students in Lunch and Learn clearly responded to this way of learning.

This way of teaching and learning is messy. There is no clear cut path or structure that can be controlled because the students are driving their own learning. They are connecting new ideas and experiences to their existing knowledge and forming a new understanding. That might mean that classrooms would have to have the resources and materials needed to bring individualized learning to meet the students where they're at and not to the whole class using rote learning with limited student engagement.

Belief in Yourself

Being creative demands that you will not be understood by the world at large. Your innovative ideas might not work or be wrong. Some children are afraid of those feelings. Even adults don't like to put themselves outside of their comfort zone. Fear can be crippling. I have certainly endured many of my own fears of being embarrassed or looking unintelligent. But it is our fears that keep us from shining the light that is within all of us. We all have talents that exist inside of us. Can you imagine how dreary our lives would be without our true selves being present in it? Let your light shine. You were put on this earth to carry a legacy and a responsibility to future generations. Just like the seeds that come from the trees, we are here to spread that which lies within us to transform ourselves and the world. Here are some steps to help you believe in yourself:

◊ Know *how* you're smart. Like Aristotle told us, "Know Thyself." What do you care about? Which intelligences did you fall into using the chart in the previous chapter?

◊ Use *affirmation* to practice positive talk to yourself each day—all the energy, power, and confidence is within you. You can access this through meditation, journaling, prayer, etc.

◊ Be a both an *observer* and a *participant* in life. Listen to the wisdom of others, notice the world around you. Make observations and begin a dialogue. Take action by participating in things that matter to you. Your actions will build your self-belief muscle.

Overcome Fear

Establish what is real and what is "False Evidence that Appears Real." Forgive yourself, and let go of any feelings of failure or mistakes you have made. We are all human and as stated we are not perfect by any means. Live in the present, not the past.

When you feel fearful or frozen, choose to just take the next step. Don't think too far ahead, just keep moving forward. It helps to listen to your own small, still voice of strength and choose to ignore the thoughts and actions of others that want to keep you down.

"If you can't fly then run, if you can't run then walk, if you can't walk then crawl, but whatever you do, you have to keep moving forward."
~ Martin Luther King Jr.

Continue to Grow

Learning is messy because it requires us to learn something, try it out, fail in some areas and then learn some more. If you approach learning with the intent that you might make a mistake and fail then it will be easier for you to put yourself out there. Know that there will be people along the way that will criticize and make fun of what you are doing. This should help you to know that in order to grow internally we have to endure this uncomfortable part. Growing takes lots of courage and support. Look around at your inner circle of friends and family. Do they support or criticize your ideas? Do they bring love and understanding to your efforts?

After a disappointing failure in my personal life, I turned to my creativity for healing. My friends were encouraging me to take yoga classes but I am a maker at heart. I needed to use my hands to "make" something. There was talk that knitting was becoming the new yoga. I dabbled in sewing in high school fashion class and I cross stitched some blankets and wall hangings while pregnant with my sons, but I never thought of knitting back then.

Near my home, I found a local yarn shop and I feverishly took any and all classes to learn to knit. They were very patient with me because my energy level was not matching the quietness of knitting. It was in those quiet moments of the many stitches that I worked through my pain, my feelings of failure. It was also in those quiet moments that I practiced slow living. My life in the past was filled with work, going to college classes at night, driving my children to after school activities and then the cooking, laundry, cleaning and lesson plans/marking papers until late at night. Knitting was like meditation and making in one. I found myself lost in thoughts of the painful past. As I continued to knit each item and finished that beautiful piece my thoughts started to change. My thoughts became hopeful, happy and my inner child started to come to the surface.

I made blankets, baby cardigans, and even a sweater. My family was shocked as I never showed an interest in knitting. I didn't stop with knitting. I would venture out and take classes and workshops in painting, sewing and even punch rug. I remember driving an hour to find a fabric shop to learn how to make a Caftan dress. What a wonderful experience. It was through these experiences that you make human connections and feel that you are not alone in your "making." Others just like you have a passion too. I was growing and changing and becoming confident in my ability. Could it be that my grandmother's sewing abilities have transferred to me? Or was it that I gave myself the opportunity to venture into the unknown without any expectation except to learn something new. I will admit however that after having feelings of complete failure I wasn't afraid to try something new. The only way out of these defeated feelings was UP! LOOK UP! You'll read more about the importance of looking up in Chapter 9.

Learning is messy!

We bring our vulnerability and hope that it takes flight—like a kite string—we have to have the opportunity to let go and let the string out so we can fly. Know that we might crash along the way every now and then but eventually we fly so high that others will tug us a little to make sure we are okay in our flight.

So keep the space open for messiness—a classroom, a room in your house, your brain as it takes ideas and imaginative thought to flight. There might be glue, paint, broken crayons, pieces of fabric and mess all around but it is in those moments of messiness that we find our way to healing if we let go of judgement and embrace creativity.

CREATIVE CUES

Breath deep and relax into the making. Pick up any-thing—a pencil, a paintbrush with paints, a needle and thread with some fabric and relax into the making. Don't worry about what it's going to become. Let your mind relax and see where it takes you. Hearing yourself think and create is exciting and it will also reveal things to you that you've been thinking about or worried about. Trust in yourself and your making.

Let go of any judgements or negative thoughts. Push aside negative thoughts or judgements and practice positive talk. Find one or two things you are proud of in your making and creating. If you make a mistake, trust that you will adjust it, scrap it and try again, or come up with a solution to keep moving forward.

Healing Hands

Find fabric scraps and thread to mend something togeth-er—cut, shape, and work into a patchwork of healing. With each cut up scrap attach it to a difficult situation and pair it with a new situation and start stitching. Continue until you no longer have a painful memory to "stitch up." Feel free to meditate and pray as you go. You could use old T-shirts and recycled garments.

Warm and Fuzzy

Sometimes making something completely different from what used to be can have a way of clearing up the messiness in our lives. Growing up means letting go of things we loved. If you child had a favorite sweater, then can make something new. Cut up an old sweater and see if you can make some hand warmers or cut up the chest area to make a "Stuffy Fluffy." See the Creativity Break after Chapter 8.

We are all in this together. The community of makers expands worldwide and we have wonderful people who are happy to share their knowledge and creativity. Find a local shop or community center and see if they are offering any classes that you might be interested in pursuing. If you cannot find anything locally reach out on social media. Communication through Instagram and Facebook has increased people's confidence to not be afraid to share their talents with the world. There are lots of courses online and webinars you can watch to connect yourself with creative communities. Share your "making" with our Creative Community on Instagram at #givemebackmycrayons.

Embracing Messy at Home

Embracing messiness at home can seem overwhelming if the area in which they play is the central location where the family comes in and out. Messiness can involve many parts that don't seem to be at all coordinated until the final stages and it somehow comes together. How does that happen? Let's say for example a child decided they were going to take their dolls and action heroes and set up a scene from their imagination. This play might involve moving furniture, collecting pillows, maybe even getting cardboard and paper with some tape to hold up the structure. During the play the house will become unsettled because their creative mind is forming and shaping the vision in which they imagined. Along the way, their learning changes because the reality of their decisions either worked or failed in which case they need to adjust and try again! This then leads them to transition away from the messiness towards their finished idea.

Embracing Messy at School

At school, messiness is not seen in the physical sense but in the creation of a body of work whether it be a writing piece, a mathematical problem or acting out a scene in a group project. It is the small moments that lead up to the finished project. The moments in between where the student cannot see the end result until they work and mold, try it out, erase the answer, modify the sentence, add more ideas and walla—there it is. Learning emerges!

CREATIVITY BREAK

Create Hand Warmers from a Sweater:

1. Measure the distance from your elbow to the middle of your palm.
2. Place those measurements onto the sleeve of the recycled sweater.
3. Be careful to leave the end of the sweater sleeve for the middle of your hand and cut only the area around the elbow.
4. Stitch the frayed ends so it doesn't unravel.
5. Decorate each sleeve (hand warmer) with fancy embroidery stitches, buttons, applique, beads, etc.
6. Have fun!

KEY #5

PUT THE PHONE AWAY

You Don't Need It

"Put down your cell phone, put everything away,
and feel your blood pulsing in you,
feel your creative impulse, feel your own spirit,
your heart, your mind.
Feel the joy of being alive and free."
~ Patti Smith

Your cell phone doesn't have the ANSWER to your happiness, YOU DO!

When I was a new mother raising my boys in the 90's I can't tell you how many presents were given that were videos. The latest Barney video and Disney tempted the family when they would release their new "digitally remastered" version of . . . we were convinced we had to own the "classics." Each movie that was released came with it a gamut of products; pajamas, sheets, toys and even wrapping paper. I admit I fell in love with every Disney movie and cartoon and as I watched them along with my boys I became a child again. We would sing the songs and act out the parts. When I hired a babysitter to watch my youngest son when I was working as a teacher, I came home one day early from work to find that my 10 month old was strapped in his car seat on the rug and facing the television watching soap operas.

At first I didn't know how to react since making a big deal of it would mean having to find another sitter in a short amount of time and I couldn't take off weeks from work. I ran to his car seat on the floor and picked him up out of the seat and into my arms. He wasn't crying or unhappy . . . he had this far away stare which shook me to the bones. I swayed and rocked him as I asked her why she had placed my son in the seat. She told me he was crawling everywhere and she needed a break.

My mind raced thinking this was probably a routine. I had nightmares and fears for months afterwards imagining my son crying and being strapped in because it was too much for her. I'd thought I would be coming home and seeing them play with stacking cups or making music with the xylophone or just interacting with the various toys that children grow developmentally; push and pull toys, sensory based toys and all the developmentally appropriate toys that I purchased because that was my profession, understanding the education of children. Instead she was unable to take care of him physically which resulted in my son staring at the TV for hours each day.

I was so upset and my feelings of guilt as a working mother took over. I was already spending hours away to go to graduate school at night and now working made me feel that I was a terrible mother never spending time with my children. I thought somehow if my life was different and I could be a stay at home mom this wouldn't have happened. She never returned to my home to watch my son. I started tutoring and making extra money to place him in a Montessori daycare. Even now after all these years I get a sick feeling in my stomach when I think about it.

During my children's early school years I made time to visit their classroom and do fun projects like macaroni necklaces that would teach patterns. I volunteered to go into their elementary school and teach famous works of art through a special PTO program. After little league practices and games in the summer we would spend time at the beach and find the stars at night. If we spent time at the beach in the summer I would take along field guides that had beautiful pictures of seashells and every species imaginable.

I remember going on local trips during the summer as if I was making up for lost time during the school year. I would bring them to the zoo, aquariums, historical buildings and each summer I would have them keep a journal almost like a scrap book where they could glue their movie ticket and write about their experiences. It was the most precious moments because there were no distractions of TV or technology. We took in all the sights and sounds and learning experiences we could find. It's amazing how many free events exist for parents and children in community centers, local and national parks and of course through the local library. But it was those winter months that would force us to stay inside and as my sons grew older each year it was a tug of war competing with video games whether it was handheld or attached to a TV. It certainly was easier to disconnect from technology during the summer months.

Technology Takes the Stage Front and Center

As my boys grew older and started to engage in sports and after school activities, their time with technology decreased. They would ride their bikes through the neighborhood to play a pick-up game of baseball. They became fascinated with collecting. They collected everything from baseball cards, funny bones (plastic monsters) every kind of ball (bouncy balls, baseballs, softballs, soccer balls, Lacrosse balls, basketballs, even the balls that you sit on with a handle at the top and bounce around). They were very active, so having a football catch in the street or playing basketball seemed first place in their lives. We were lucky to have a neighborhood of kids.

Then middle school came and everyone in 6th and 7th grade had gotten a cell phone. Parents at the time were projecting their fear about not having their child be able to contact them if they needed to after school. Mom's would gather during a sporting event and talk about how comfortable they felt when their child called them on the phone to let them know they were at practice and if the coach practiced for a longer period of time they weren't outside waiting. They would add how convenient it was to get in touch with their kids and they could check in on them from time to time.

This idea gripped our town and soon every kid in middle school had a cell phone. We tried to hold off and in 8th grade our boys received their first cell phone. I have to admit that as a working mom it was comforting to know that I can reach them and find out what they were doing and if they walked home safely. Why was I so worried? Our town was a safe place to live yet the fears of others were making me feel uneasy. Anywhere they ventured out with their friends to the movies, malls, neighborhood stores, it was an easy way to get in touch with them. But just like it took over our school community, it took over our family. No longer were we together in conversation and presence. Now everyone was in a separate room watching their own show or playing a video game. It became a huge distraction to our family and time together.

What happened to our time of playing board games, putting Legos together and puzzles? Sports were already taking over the television and now the cell phone was taking over what little time we had once homework and dinner were over. What happened to our family time? What happened to the silly, imaginative times that were spent creating games and stories?

As video games were exploding in children's conversations they were in every storefront, advertisement and now were a section in the magazine area of the bookstores. Books and websites were popping up on how to crack the game. It became an obsession that even when my kids got together with their friends, video games were the main focus. They were trapped in a world of artificial reality. Instead of growing their friendships they were growing their high score. They couldn't wait to come home and tell us how they wanted to get the gaming system that their friends had. You can imagine the everyday banter of convincing us of all the reasons why they should have this latest and greatest system. I thought this should be put into an argumentative essay for their English teacher. She could've used this platform to teach persuasive writing not to mention comparative research.

There were many times that I took away their video games as they were unable to control their use. I would come home from work to find that their homework wasn't done and they were playing video games for quite some time. Tests that they needed to study for where the books were out and opened on the kitchen table but they were up and down running to play, shut it off study a few more paragraphs then up again. They always had a reason why this worked for them. Of course when their grades came in or report cards were issued the effects were real. Technology was taking over their lives.

First it was taking away the controller for a day or two.

Finally the rule in the house became no video games Monday through Friday. It was amazing how homework, studying for tests and projects started to get done in a timely way. Schoolwork and family came first and we were going to hold our ground on that. There were times when they would take their phone out to text back their friends and I would again have to have the conversation of protecting family time. It has been a struggle over the years. I still to this day become very upset when I see precious family moments robbed by cell phone use.

I was having a lovely dinner one night with a friend, when I noticed this family of 4 sitting at the table. The husband was talking with his two boys and the mother was on her phone attempting to catch up on social media and be in the conversation with her family. What I couldn't understand is how she never looked up from her phone She continued to have a conversation with her boys as they attempted to talk with her. They didn't have cell phones but just stared at her as she continued to talk with them and never looked up. She was unaware of their facial expressions of disappointment because she just never put the phone away.

As parents, we are the role models. We are the ones they look to for comfort, guidance and support. Our body language, actions, facial expressions, and tone of voice are what they see and mimic, especially under the age of 5. Nothing is more important than the time you spend with the ones we love. We as parents are certainly not perfect but we have to get a handle on our tech use and put the phone away.

Technology Stifles Our Own Ideas

I'll tell you, you're far more creative without the phone. In an instant you can generate any image and copy any Pinterest perfect picture, but there is no intrinsic value that compares to when it comes from within.

I had a friend who wanted to make her daughter's birthday special by baking and decorating cupcakes. Instead of trusting her inner creativity, she went onto Pinterest to look for the perfect cupcake design. When she tried to make it look like the perfect picture on the screen, it turned out just the opposite. It didn't look anything like the picture and it was a disaster. She didn't trust her own creativity. Time was running out and she couldn't run around to stores. She took a deep breath and thought about how much her daughter loved dogs. She baked brownies instead and cut them to look like doggie bones. She used her creativity to decorate the brownies and in her daughter's eyes they were perfect because thought, care and love went into it.

Yes, the phone can give us immediate ideas but it also boxes us in and makes us focus on what's being presented so then we will view it through that lens.

I was recently at a professional development workshop offered by the Count Basie Theatre called Mind Aligned. It's a way to teach Creative Teaching Strategies in all content areas. They presented the group of educators a picture of the famous artwork by Cornelis Saftlever, "An Enchanted Cellar with Animals (1655-1670)." We were asked to think about what we see and notice. We stared at it looking for similarities and differences. We used our synthesizing skills to think about "the big idea." We were asked to connect our ideas to something else we have learned or a time in our life when we've experienced or seen something similar?

When we had a chance to talk about it, we were amazed at all the different viewpoints, but it was interesting when they mentioned a movie from our childhood, our viewpoint of the artwork took on a whole new meaning. Our creativity came to a halt because we were only focused on the connection to the movie and nothing else. Our creativity was impacted by someone else's viewpoint.

Although video games were in my children's lives and still are to this day with the Fortnite takeover, my sons have gained a perspective of the time and place for them. They have taken responsibility to be in charge and monitor their use. Even though they are in their twenties as of this writing, I still have conversations with them about putting their phones away when in the company of family visits and events. I continue to talk to my sons about their video gaming and they still roll their eyes as they did when they were in high school. I will never stop communicating to them the importance of being present in the lives of the ones you love. We deserve their attention and presence.

If you're not sure about what to do with your child's obsession with cell phones and electronic devices, the American Academy of Pediatrics has given us a roadmap. The information below was part of Children and Media. Tips for Parents written from two AAP Policies, "Media Use in School-Aged Children and Adolescents" and "Media and Young Minds." They were also drawn from the proceedings of the AAP Sponsored Growing Up Digital: Media Research Symposium, a gathering of media experts, researchers and pediatricians held in 2015 to address new developments in research and their impact on children.

Putting Away the Phone at Home

In order to help your child put their phone away, you have to model what that looks like. Opening up discussions on why it's important to put devices and phones away can help our children understand the importance of the protected time. Time moves us through the day with various commitments and routines but it is the mindfulness of the time together that will be the time we remember the most even if it's only a short amount of time. It needs to be "phone free."

Putting away your phone at home can be a commitment as a family to protect your time together. "Family time" can only happen if all family members place their devices out of sight in a location far away from where the family gathers or has meals. Instead of spending hours scrolling through posts and messages on a phone, families can have time together to socialize and communicate about their lives, their dreams, their difficulties. Looking at one another instead of looking down. Making eye contact and picking up on each other's facial expressions can reveal just what each family member is going through. Maybe problems can be solved sooner instead of waiting for it to come to a boil. "Are you okay? It looks like something is bothering you? Do you want to talk about it?" can be a perfect start to eliminating a bad day.

Putting Away the Phone at School

At school, phones are usually put away in lockers and prohibited from being in class. In some high schools, phones are collected and put in a basket on the teacher's desk and picked up on the way out. I sometimes think that students just see everyone else on their phones so they retreat to going on it even if they might have an idea to do something else—they would need to convince their friends to get off their device too. This might take some strength and courage. Should we model what that might look like? Should we have students role model the dialogue and discussions to persuade their friends to put the phone away.

What if you hired a babysitter who stayed on her phone instead of interacting with your child? Who thought it was more important to watch her favorite TV show instead of encouraging your child to play? What if they strapped your child into a portable car seat and faced him to stare at the TV for hours and was too small to ask for help?

My heart sank the moment I realized that I hired a babysitter who didn't find joy to be around children. Who replaced the joy of play with forcing a child to be still and quiet? Can we as adults be asked to sit still and quiet for long periods of time for something we don't want to do? Is it too late for our kids to get back their childhood if it means to put their phone away in order to get it back? I say we need to awaken and take back our children's innocence and childhood. To give them an environment of child-like play, imaginative conversations and moments of curiosity. Instead of watching your child fall victim to the pull of technology and corporations who have convinced us that they are born digital, let's provide them with uninterrupted play with as many different experiences that lead to life skills and innovative thinking.

We cannot expect our children to unlock the creativity within if we allow them to spend most of their time pushing buttons, scrolling and hitting "like" in response to a picture, video or event. The text message can wait and the sky will not fall if they don't respond to their friends' posts.

Look up—there's a whole world to be noticed. The colors, textures of nature at different times of the year; the sounds of nature on a spring day; the smell of a woodland forest on a fall day. Take a drive and stop along lookout points because sometimes when we travel even a small distance from home, we return a different person. Renewed and our lens in which we look at life seems changed somehow—in a good way. Just look up!

When the device is away, creativity can come out and play.

What To Do? AAP Helps Us Figure It Out

In a world where children are "growing up digital," it's

important to help them learn healthy concepts of digital use and citizenship. Parents play an important role in teaching these skills. Here are a few tips from the AAP to help families manage the ever-changing digital landscape.

Media Plan

Make your own family media use plan. Media should work for you and within your family values and parenting style. When used inappropriately, media can displace many important activities such as face-to-face interaction, family-time, outdoor-play, exercise, unplugged downtime and sleep.

Your Child's Environment

Treat media as you would any other environment in your child's life. The same parenting guidelines apply in both real and virtual environments. Set limits. Kids need and expect them. Know your children's friends, both online and off. Know what platforms, software and apps your children are using, what sites they are visiting on the web and what they are doing online.

Encourage Playtime

Set limits and encourage playtime. Media use, like all other activities, should have reasonable limits. Unstructured and offline play stimulates creativity. Make unplugged playtime a daily priority, especially for very young children.

Watch Together

Screen time shouldn't always be a long time. Co-view, co-play, and co-encourage with your children when they are using screens. It encourages social interactions, bonding and learning. Play a video game with your kids. It's a good way to demonstrate good sportsman and gaming etiquette. Watch a show with them; you will have the opportunity to introduce and share your own life experiences and perspectives, and guidance. Don't just monitor children online, interact with them—you can understand what they are doing and be a part of it.

You Are the Role Model

Be a good role model. Teach and model kindness and good manners online. Children are great mimics so limit your own media use. In fact, you'll be more available for and connected with your children if you're interacting, hugging, playing with them rather than simply staring at a screen.

Face-To-Face

Know the value of face-to-face communication. Very young children learn best through two-way communication. Engaging in back-and-forth "talk time" is critical for language development. Conversations can be face-to-face, or if necessary, by video chat with a traveling parent or far-away grandparent. Research has shown that it's that "back-and-forth conversations" that improves language skills—much more so than "passive" listening or one-way interaction with a screen.

Limit Time On Devices

Limit digital media for your youngest family members. Avoid digital media for toddlers younger than 18 to 24 months other than video chatting. For children 18 to 24 months, watch digital media with them because they learn from watching and talking with you. Limit screen use for preschool children, ages 2-5, to just 1 hour a day of high quality programming.

Again co-viewing is best when possible and for young children they learn best when they are re-taught in the real world what they just learned through a screen. So if Ernie just taught the letter D, you can reiterate this later when you are having dinner or spending time with your child.

Tech-Free Zones

Create tech-free zones. Keep family mealtimes, other family and social gatherings, and children's bedrooms screen free. Turn off televisions that you aren't watching, because background TV can get in the way of face-to-face time with kids. Recharge devices overnight, outside your child's bedroom to help avoid the temptation to use them when they should be sleeping. These changes encourage more family time, healthier eating habits and better sleep.

Technology Isn't A Pacifier

Don't use technology as an emotional pacifier. Media can be very effective in keeping kids calm and quiet, but it should not be the only way they learn to calm down. Children need to be taught how to identify and handle strong emotions, come up with activities to manage boredom, or calm down through breathing, talking about ways to solve the problem, and finding other strategies for channeling emotions.

Which Apps are best?

More than 80,000 apps are labeled as educational, but little research has demonstrated their actual quality. Products pitched as "interactive should require more than "pushing and swiping." Look to organizations like Common Sense Media (www.commonsensemedia.org) for reviews about age-appropriate apps, games and programs to guide you in making the best choices for your children.

CREATIVE CUES

Creativity can lead the way in helping families and children see their way through this stronghold. There are so many ways to disconnect and start enjoying your family time and help your children navigate the technology pull. If families decide to put the phone away and devote tech free time there are lots of things to do.

Human Connection

Gather some neighbors and friends for a potluck dinner each month. Each family brings a dish to feed four people. You can decide on a theme and the dishes can be made to match the theme. You can set up activities inside or outside depending on the weather to get each family to interact with each other. Instead of the kids playing separately from the adults you can involve everyone. Playing games like Charades and/or Pictionary for inside and kickball or scavenger hunt for outside creates team building and memorable moments.

Community Help

Gathering your family and friends for a good cause will always have its rewards that technology cannot match. Giving of your time to help others in need or just revitalizing your hometown can make all the difference. Usually when traumatic events happen or unforeseen weather hits neighborhoods and towns, cities and states rally to help out the cause. But what about the everyday things that can be done for your neighborhood. There are so many organizations that can use our help to improve the lives in our communities. Shelters, pantries, and animal rescue sites are always in need of volunteers to help.

As Ghandi's words ring throughout the world, "Be the Change You Wish to See in the World," there is no better time in our world today than to show our children how to be involved with volunteering and social justice programs.

Jeanne Segal, PhD has written many books and articles on the benefits of volunteering stating, "volunteer work can help you find meaning and can be a relaxing, energizing escape from your day-today routine of work, school or family commitments. Volunteering also provides you with renewed creativity, motivation, and vision that can carry over into your personal and professional life." There are so many different places that would appreciate any time you have to give for a good cause.

World Volunteer Web suggests you think about these things before you get started to make sure it's going to give you the best experience for you and your family:

◊ What causes are important to you?

◊ How much time can you devote?

◊ Would you like to work with adults, children, animals or from home?

Art Therapy

Art therapy has emerged in the face of many children in schools who suffer with anxiety and depression. Art therapy is defined by the American Art Therapy Association as a means to allow for creative expressive that can overcome the limitations of language. If an idea or emotion is too difficult or painful, then drawing, painting, sculpting, coloring, sewing, collaging and many different areas of visual arts can help combat the inability to talk about it. According to Doreen Meister, MA, MFT, a mindfulness-based, expressive art and depth psychotherapist in Oakland, CA, a benefit of art therapy is its ability to calm the nervous system: "When we're focused on creating, our attention shifts . . . the simple act of creative expression connects us with an inner sense of vitality."

We have seen the amount of mindfulness activities that include coloring pages for adults and children. These coloring pages have boosted children's self-esteem and provided a way to improve confidence with each color selection. Whether coloring inside or outside the lines, there is a freedom of expression and that in itself will spark creative thoughts to occur. But remember for an activity to be deemed "Art Therapy" it must be done with a licensed Art Therapist.

Fill the Tank Well

I remember the year we picked *Energy Bus* by Jon Gordon. The parents left our book club feeling renewed and had a strong handle on their thoughts about their life and future ahead of them. The session was filled with discussions about people we allow "on our bus" to ride the journey of life together. We examined our attitudes towards others and ourselves. We made clear goals for our family and lives that we would live it out with a purpose. What family decisions were draining us of our energy and which ones filled our tank? Certainly excessive cell phone use and how to control the "devices" that were robbing their kids of childhood experiences.

Observe and Notice

Wherever you go you are bound to find someone on these devices. Have you ever stopped to check out just how many people are on their phones as they are walking in the streets, malls, and grocery stores? Try it! You'll be amazed at the number you come up with.

CREATIVITY BREAK

Find a card, postcard, notecard, or blank piece of paper. Write a letter to someone you would normally text. Put the letter in the mail and be sure to ask for one in return.

KEY #6

TRUST YOURSELF

No Instructions Necessary

"It took me a whole lifetime to paint like a child."
~ Pablo Picasso

It was Christmas morning and my boys were opening their presents with the whole family. There was wrapping paper everywhere and excited shouts. "Let me see! What did you get?" All the cousins lifted their gifts to show and then tore into the next one. My parents always made Christmas special in that they would wrap their grandchildren's presents and then place them in this enormous sack as if it came straight off of Santa's sled. The grandkids would scream and feverishly open each one.

After all the excitement settled, it was on to picking a toy to open and play with. My son Gregory loved Legos and so he was happy to get an assortment pack where every shape, size, color and accessories were included. There was no instruction book and it was only his imagination and creativity at work. He couldn't wait to dive in and start building. His uncle watched as he took all the blocks out and started to build. Sharing in the excitement his uncle started to build alongside him and interact with the play, but somehow the play turned into:

"No, this piece goes over here."

"See these wheels, these go under this one."

Gregory got up and left the set on the rug beside the Christmas tree and grabbed something else to play with. My son took out a superhero figurine (Batman) and started to create a scene in the sky as he moved his arm in large swirls. Batman could fly and the stories were alive as he chanted, "I will get you."

I placed his Lego pieces back into the bucket and returned it to the sack of toys. Today Gregory still loves to build with Legos, but doesn't deviate from the instruction book.

Lego Lesson

Messages you send with your words and actions. To a child it's just an imaginary time spent building, creating and forming ideas. It's not a set of rules, with boundaries. There are no directions in a big bucket of Legos or Duplo blocks. There might be warnings of small pieces and toddlers but not on the creativity. You cannot give creativity boundaries. Even in the quiet times, creativity will emerge. Even when a child imagines the car or truck he is building where the wheel is not asymmetrical, it is still a car or a truck to them. Instead of putting your spin or judgement on the "right and wrong" way to do things you can simply say, "I can see you're busy building something . . . can you tell me about it?" Trust me . . . children love to talk about their creative minds at work. Your response will either shut them down or encourage them to continue.

Unfortunately my son was turned off to playing openly as he felt his imaginary play was interrupted by his uncle trying to show him the correct way to build. Trust takes a faith and a confidence in oneself and others. You have the ability to build trust in your child by giving them emotional support, loving them even when they make mistakes and communicating that in words and in actions. If our children aren't given respect for their ideas and even in the face of failures or mistakes then they will have difficulty trusting themselves and others.

At home children see and hear situations that either build their relationships or tear them down. They usually know when an adult is honest or when they're lying. They can tell by words and body language if their friends are "trustworthy." You know those middle school and high school years when you experienced a betrayal of a friendship. Those are the best lessons and perfect opportunities to discuss trusting others and yourself. It is in those times when your child, young adult will have to find the strength within and bravery to face those situations or conflicts. How do they do it? Confidence comes from years of a combination of positive self-talk, love and support from family, encouragement to remain curious, and praising perseverance in the face of difficulty.

Even at school, the environment and community must commit to a positive culture. Students in school must see themselves as curious and resilient. It is important for schools to praise students not just for being "smart," but for tackling a challenge even if they fail, there is a reflection on how that mistake helped them improve or grow. When children trust themselves, they will be curious and not afraid of making mistakes because they know it will reveal a truth, a direction, or a new idea.

Instructions are necessary for certain items in our life that might need repair or help us to get things up and running. If a light turns on in the car you turn to the owner's manual in the car. If you buy your child a present that requires parts that have to be put together in order to make it work (even if it is Christmas Eve) then having that manual is a saving grace. However instructions can hinder us sometimes too. I can tell you my memory of getting place to place is far worse today as I rely my Waze app and Google maps to get around.

In today's world you can find instructions for just about anything and it's only a click away; YouTube video tutorial, Wiki How step-by-step, you can learn how to bake the perfect cake, how to prune a rose, how to build a treehouse, how to fish, how to sew, how to knit, how to draw the perfect cartoon character or play the perfect "Ode to Joy" on the piano.

The downside to this is we don't have to think anymore.

We don't have to use our creativity to come up with sewing patterns or your own song on the piano. Figuring out how to thread a needle isn't that hard but they figured it out. Children shouldn't have to rely on instructions in every aspect of their lives. They even are given instructions on how to spend their time, being scheduled from morning till night.

Growing up we didn't have a plan each day. We went to school, came home and did our homework and played outside until dinner was ready. My friends and I didn't have scheduled play dates. We played pick-up games with our neighborhood friends. Everything was decided on the spot. If we played in teams we divided up each other with captains that selected us from a line up. We always waited to see who would be picked first and even dreading if we were picked last.

We knew who the neighborhood bully was and we always found a way to stick together and help each other out when trouble came rolling around. We were a pack, a group of kids bound together by geographic lines but tied together with a sense of purpose: to develop and grow into the men and women we were meant to be.

We had different personalities, habits and routines. We didn't mind those differences because we just wanted to be kids, using our imaginations and having the freedom to be a kid.

We had a group of boys in the neighborhood that loved to "build" things. At that time, homes were being built and there were scraps of wood laying around. We had an idea to meet in the wooded area and bring our dad's hammer and nails. I searched the garage and grabbed my supplies. We all met in the woods and there lay a pile of 2 by 4's and plywood.

Somehow no one asked where they got it or how it appeared there we just had a mission—to build a fort. Yes, a fort in the woods away from our parents and school. We tried multiple times to nail in pieces of wood into the tree. We held up pieces as Phil and Tommy yelled out what supplies we needed or "raise it up higher."

We had jeans or "dungarees" as we knew it, scrappy hair, sneakers worn out and scuffs everywhere, tube socks with different colored stripes and T-shirts with iron on letters and iron on pictures. We were trying out our design ideas. The ladder was easy because we had background knowledge of the construction as we've seen ladders in playgrounds and in our homes when our parents changed lightbulbs etc. But building a floor in between tree limbs.

It took us about a month but it was our own creation. Sometimes our planning didn't go so well, nailed in pieces of wood for stairs to climb up broke if we had multiple people climbing up at once like a race around the track. If anyone rough housed while in the fort the plywood would crack and break, especially the pieces that acted as walls. It was always patched up and repaired.

Together we learned many lessons: how to communicate with each other, making our directions and instructions for building; we collaborated when we shared our ideas for design; we failed multiple times pulling out the nails and repositioning the beams to hold up the structure. But it was our structure; our imperfect fort . . . our hideaway where we could laugh, dream and solve our silly problems that seemed so big at the time.

Tree House Lesson

That tree house helped us to trust one another and ourselves. It wasn't a contest or competition, we had a mission and it was to build a safe space in the woods. That treehouse deepened our trust with ourselves and each other. We had to be confident enough to face a challenge knowing we might fail or make mistakes (hopefully without any one of us getting hurt). We had to persevere if we did run into a problem like the ladder collapsing. But most importantly it taught us to respect and trust each other and our abilities. We knew who to call on for the different parts of creating this treehouse. We did our best and trusted our abilities but made sure we laughed along the way. That was part of motivation to be creative—finding the joy in the making, the moments that bring you surprise and excitement. The thrill of the small moments coming together until you all decide, "That's it! That's exactly what we imagined it to be!" We didn't have Pinterest back then and no one put judgement on it because there wasn't a person or platform that forced us to compare it to. It was our treehouse—imperfect and beautiful. It brought us closer together that summer because we didn't give up on each other. We didn't give up on our creativity.

Living Instruction Free

We continued to live instruction free. If we all gathered in the school yard with our bikes then we made up games like cops and robbers with teams. We had to find the stolen "object." We would chase each other on bikes and laugh in triumph if we were able to find it. We used our inference skills and process of elimination to figure out who was hiding the stolen object.

When we hung around on a summer night in the playground area my best friend and I would make up songs. We would laugh and continue singing. There was even a song we made up about Ritz Crackers. Her mom was the neighborhood piano teacher and music was an important part of my childhood and still is today.

As I grew older, time for fort building dwindled. I'd spent years living by instructions. School work, working, marriage . . . but when I was expecting Gregory, my creative energy spiked. I was going to throw out those instructions and create something that was all me! I remember thinking I should "make" something for the baby's room. So I went out to find a blanket that I would eventually cross stitch baby motif's. I loved relaxing in the making and feeling the baby kick. My happiness and joy of creativity was coming back to life so I found another project, an ABC framed picture that I would stitch animals and objects around the letters.

Then I had a wonderful idea . . . what if each member of my family put together a square representing one letter of the alphabet and together would be a wall hanging quilt that the baby could look at and learn his letters as well as enjoy the beautiful handmade work. The family was so excited. I mailed or handed a square piece of muslin with a red letter. There were no instructions except they could draw, paint, stitch a symbol or object that begins with that letter.

The results were amazing!

My aunts and uncles met at my grandmother's house and they had a creativity pop-up session. My aunt who was always crafty brought the fabric markers, paints, etc. and off they went. I received the most beautiful handmade work that wasn't perfect but it was made with pure love. Each picture made you dream and imagine and the colors and textures were astonishing.

A Knight from King Arthur you would think would be for K but it was Uncle Ed who would create the image for "Quest", Pony by Uncle Ken, and even my brother Tom traced his hand for H. There were of course Crayons for the letter C from my dad and my Aunt Dolly's husband Vinny loved drawing Donald and Daisy Duck. Patched fabric made into hearts from Uncle Anthony and a terry-cloth textured umbrella from my childhood friend ReRe.

This beautiful quilt was displayed at the Christening celebration and on the wall where his changing table was placed. My son would look at it and point to it and touch it year after year throughout his childhood. When my youngest son was born four years later I dove into making him his own quilt and pillow for his crib.

Creativity was back and my soul was alive and happy again.

When I see many children in the schools today, there seems to be a distant look in their eyes. An emptiness and passivity that keeps growing every year. It's almost like they're waiting for instructions to be given to them. They give up their freedom to think for fear they will be wrong or fail or say something that their friends will make fun of.

Do we as adults feel that way in our workplace or at meetings?

Do we hesitate to put out an idea that seems silly or will be judged by our peers?

I would rather work with a team that questions and pushes each other to think and see differently than a team of people who nod yes at everything you say and do.

How do we as parents and educators reach these passive learners? Put them in situations where they need to use their creativity and imagination. Infuse some aspect of the arts into the curriculum.

I will go into more detail in Chapter 8, "One Size Doesn't Fit All," but for now here is an example. When I was teaching 3rd grade and the Social Studies curriculum was about 50 states, I was hoping to get them excited to retain all the information and geography needed to understand this content. I had to follow textbook lessons that were accompanied by a workbook that provided worksheets that students had to fill out to show their understanding of the different concepts and vocabulary. The students body language changed when

the subject would begin. They didn't want to sit at their desks like they were at a job filling out paperwork and handing it in to be checked.

I had to think of something that would spark their curiosity and imagination. What if the study of birds could help assist them in gathering information about the various 50 states? Wasn't there a state bird in every state? I knew I had to find a way to make learning real to them and have them see that the content can be used to understand other disciplines. We began to read and notice birds in our community and around the United States. We set up a bird feeder outside the window of my classroom and decided to track the birds that would visit the bird feeder each day.

There were no instructions, no teacher manual, no sense of right or wrong. We were charged with a motivation to immerse ourselves to resolve the curiosity that was within us. What kind of bird is that? Where does it live? How is it the same or different than other birds?

I found out about a program called Project Feeder Watch. This program allowed us to send our observations to Cornell University's Ornithology Lab. The scientists received our list of birds and how many came to our feeder each week. We enjoyed watching House Sparrows and European Starlings at our bird feeder. We made charts and graphs to analyze our data. We took turns filling up the feeder with seed and suet. Students studied the bird's size, shape, wingspan, nests, migration and food. The learning experience was beyond what I could've planned or imagined.

The learning instructions were nowhere to be found. In fact the students continued to share with each other their learning during lunch, recess, on Monday mornings after the weekend—somehow birds were on their minds and they noticed them everywhere they went.

What if I could take them birdwatching?

I raised money and wrote a grant for a field trip to Huber Woods. Sam the Bird man was hesitant to take a group of 2nd graders out into the fields expecting they had limited knowledge. I was told, "Let's bring them in for a slide show and a lecture first." I went along with this notion but in my mind I knew he would be amazed with my students once he met them. I gave parents the opportunity to come along and meet us there so we didn't have to pay for another bus. I also found a way to collect some binoculars through my friends and family.

Sam the Birdman was amazed at the response from the students when he projected the slide show of the birds that live in the county park Huber Woods. Their hands feverishly raised in excitement calling out the names of the birds they could easily identify. I often wonder why "Field Guides" are not part of a student's textbook requirements. I would strongly advise buying used or new Field Guides for all areas of Science.

Sam agreed to take my class out on a Bird Watching walk. He explained how to use the binoculars and we were off. The student's experienced finding blue robin eggs and their respect for nature increased. We came back to our class-

room with a renewed sense of learning. We published our own book "All About Birds" which resides in the school library to this day.

How can you write instructions for all of these things? You have to trust your creative spirit that resides within.

Children need to see that our learning is connected it's not separated by subject. It's all related to one another. Next holiday coming up don't buy a kit with instructions for putting the perfect Gingerbread House together or pumpkin carving kit. Give them a chance and support them when they are doubting the ideas that are coming out. Even Christmas, children need to have their own creative spirit.

The Instructions I Longed For

Year after year I would infuse creativity into my lessons, projects, grants, curriculum writing, workshops and the educational community at large. But my personal life was suffering. I had grown up two wonderful sons who were the center of my life. So much that I would give up everything to be around anything to do in their lives. If we were at a baseball field or a basketball tournament, the day was engulfed. Work gobbled up my days and weekends along with my children's activities.

I remember getting home from work on a Friday night and thinking should I wait and see what the boys have planned with their friends or make plans to go out? If work felt too hectic I would feel guilty I wasn't spending enough time with my children, if their lives were out of control I would blame myself and try to figure a way to solve it.

My days were consumed in making everyone happy or at least trying to. There was no room for me. I was empty because I had given everything to my job and my kids and there was nothing left. I wasn't taking care of myself emotionally. I was living to please everyone and make them happy but I was hurting inside. But I kept going, there was no time to stop. I got really good at keeping a schedule and putting on the game face with family, neighbors, colleagues at work, and team parents. Everything appeared fine. If my boys struggled emotionally or academically I felt it too and there were times I felt so helpless.

And then there was my marriage or should I say, lack of it. We were perfect raising our children and doing the housework. We would split the chores and much of the time when I was busy with lesson planning or going to classes at night to further my education and career my husband at the time would pick up even more. Unfortunately this routine left little time for each other. The new normal was to live separately in a house full of love for our children but not for each other. No one should ever have to beg to be loved, to be seen.

As my 25 year marriage was coming to an end and my oldest son was ready to go off to college, it was the perfect storm. There were no instructions on how to deal with all the emotions and loss. My life was changing rapidly and since I had lost myself over the years with giving of myself to my career and my family, I didn't know who I was anymore.

I so badly wanted the answers, a manual, someone to tell me what to do. I had no idea how to handle this. What do you do when your heart is broken and empty? Where do you turn to when the darkness takes over? Shopping and fixing up a home was not a sound solution because it only distracts you from dealing with the emotions you don't want to face and it can suck your nest egg dry.

I went to therapy once a week. At the beginning I would just cry and be completely engulfed in waves of every emotion possible. It was difficult to talk about the pain because when you release yourself emotionally, where do you put it once it comes out? It has to find a place before it goes away and so it was part of me for a long time. I meditated and tried to do breathing exercises in an empty bedroom that was made into a quiet prayer filled space. No furniture just mats, candles, wall hangings with inspirational messages and of course pictures of the beach (my happy place).

Again there were no instructions except to trust myself in digging deep and being okay with the messiness I felt inside and out. So I continued to go to church, pray, meditate but something was still missing.

Cardinals

Along the way on this emotional journey, I would see cardinals appear in my backyard or even fly past my car as I was driving. At first I thought I was seeing things but these beautiful red birds would be everywhere. I was convinced it was a sign. People told me that cardinals were a sign that you have a visitor from Heaven.

The day of the divorce hearing in court I was sitting in my car and a red cardinal just landed on the side by the driver's side. It just stood there and stared at me and then flew away. I got through that difficult day and continued to see cardinals wherever I went. When I would tell my family they looked at me a little strange at first especially my sons, so whenever I would see one I would try to take out my camera and send pictures off to my family so they didn't think I was losing my mind. I still see some cardinals here and there but not so many now.

When I changed my place of worship I found a wonderful group of people that embraced me with open arms. I had joined the choir and singing and hearing beautiful songs each week at practice and singing at mass started to heal me in ways which were unexplainable. God had placed people in my life that would show me unconditional love and care. It was not only in my spiritual place of worship but also in the knitting and fiber community. I had always wanted to learn to knit and so during the year of the divorce proceedings I would take classes to relax and the word was that knitting was the new yoga so off I was to try it out. Remember the classes I told you about earlier? These knitting classes led me to find my creativity. From that creative journey led me to dig out my sewing machine and month after month whatever creative project I would immerse myself into made the broken pieces of my heart start to heal. I didn't cry as much anymore and my sons would tell me how much happier I seemed. My family, my spiritual community and my creative community were the main reasons I am myself today. I trusted God and I found myself again through my "making." No instruction manual could have showed me this.

My journey of healing is seen in the pastel drawing of the beach scene, hand knitted baby blankets, cardigans and the many quilts I have stitched up. One Sunday after church 5 years after my divorce, I was looking through a bin of scraps of fabric. Each fabric had a story, a tale of happiness, hope, love, joy, and even sadness. I decided to take those scraps and sew them together to make a collage that I placed on the back of my jeans jacket. I wear this jacket proudly today because without instructions for life and for living, we are continuing to "be made." Broken pieces can always be made whole again in a new and beautiful way.

You certainly don't have to be in a dark and broken place to find happiness and joy using your creativity. It's the point with which we decide to be awakened and trust the creativity that lies within.

CREATIVE CUES

Deep Breathing and Meditation

Meditation and deep breathing each day can bring you to a state of awareness and enlightenment. Find a quiet space in your home. You can dim the lights and light some candles. Sit straight up with your legs crossed on the floor using a comfortable mat or if you have back trouble you can always sit up in a comfy chair. Breathe in for 5 and then hold your breath for 5 then exhale out for 5 Repeat several times until you feel your breathing start to become natural and fluid.

Relax into the breathing without counting anymore or holding your breath. You should feel your body relaxing and calming down. Some meditation can be to think of nothing and release the mind of any and all thoughts. So that if a worry or thought about the day or what you have to do, let it be acknowledged then let it go. Setting a timer before you begin might alleviate your worry and let you relax into the meditation exercise.

Infuse Art

Art can be connected to any content area. Take for instance Math. Many students think they are not good at it or find it boring. Parents can connect the two in many ways. Let's explore geometry. Children can find simple 2-dimensional shapes all around their neighborhoods. Looking at the architecture of a building for older students can help them understand symmetry, angles, parallel lines, perpendicular lines and 3 dimensional shapes. Take an architectural walk and see how many features you can find when you look at roof lines, columns, windows and doors.

Let Positive Energy Flow

In order to let positive energy flow, many things have to be aligned. First take care of yourself each day and create an affirmation to tell yourself each morning when you wake up.

"I am strong."

"Today I am going to begin my journey towards my goal."

Try to determine if there is negative energy stopping you from being happy. Forgiving yourself and others will clear the path. Let go of hurtful memories of the past and negative feelings. You can write a letter to that person and either mail it or throw it away, but getting out your feelings is the best way to heal and let the positive energy flow. Karma will take care of everything. Miracles and signs that you are headed in the right direction will start to appear.

CREATIVITY BREAK

Take a Creative Walk

Plan some time free of distractions to walk in nature. Notice your surroundings. Listen to the sounds. Breathe in Breathe out. Use all of your senses to observe nature.

Imagine you have wings to fly around this beautiful piece of land. What would your wings look like? What could they do?

Materials: Use any of the following or combination of: Crayons, Paper, markers, paints, fabric, sticks, flexible twisty ties, tissue paper, cardboard.

Design butterfly wings

Spend some uninterrupted time with your "making." Enjoy the process. Let your imagination have the freedom to take off and may you remove judgement from this exercise. Happy Making!!

After you are done! Take time to celebrate your creativity! If you feel a story should go along with your making, write that story in your journal. If you would like to share in our creative community, post your making on Instagram: #creativewalk #givemebackmycrayons

Here you will find that although the materials were the same, the results were different because we each bring our own individual talents and thoughts to the making. We bring different life experiences that feed into our creative self. It is a true celebration of our uniqueness that we can all share these differences and see the beauty within us with no instructions necessary.

KEY #7

ENJOY THE PROCESS

It's Worth It

"It must not be forgotten that the basic law of children's creativity is that its value lies not in its results, not in the product of creation but in the process itself. It is not important what children create, but that they do create, that they exercise and implement their creative imagination."

~ Vygotsky

My younger son Gerard loved *Blue's Clues* when he was a little boy. He would sing the song, "You know me and YOU and my dog blue, WE can do ANYTHING that we want to do! Bye Bye." He would wave goodbye and race around the house. He loved to solve the clues and earn paws. At the time, there were birthday supply companies selling all sorts of paper goods and party items and of course he wanted his next birthday party to be a "Blues Clue's" party. I found a green striped sweater for his special day but it took a lot of planning to come up with the activities for his friends and cousins.

We decided to make pawprints and scatter them around the backyard. The Nocera and Bracco family put on a Reader's Theatre where all family members had parts and a song to sing. My family and I wrote the parts and brainstormed other activities for this party two months in advance. We were ready. We had comfy red chairs and a special "mailbox" made with bendable shirt boxes and decorated with construction paper and colored Duct tape. Family and friends had a wonderful time being silly and laughing to think their stage opportunity was alive again like in elementary school. The process of building, planning, creating the play and watching it come to life was priceless!

My son couldn't stop smiling all day! My heart was bursting with joy and full of love. Love of my family. Love of the creative process, and for bringing JOY to all who attended this birthday celebration. We aren't going on Broadway anytime soon and our props and setup in that backyard on a hot summer day didn't matter because, to my son, it was his wonderful, imaginative birthday party. It was the process, not the product that made all of this magic come to life.

Lost In Imagination

Have you ever watched your children play? Really play? They lose themselves in an imaginary world whether the premise be a superhero, racing cars, castles or pretending to be princesses. They can just lose themselves in just storytelling out loud.

Children look forward to spending time with their loved ones, especially their parents. Process is truly a joy when it's met with little or no expectations towards perfection. When a parent takes out a device or goes onto the computer the message is that someone else owns their creativity when in fact it's inside all along. Modeling the process means to communicate while "making" the sights and smells come alive and focusing on each part instead of the outcome. There were so many opportunities while cooking after a long day of work that my sons and I would laugh and have fun while preparing dinner. My kitchen had this peninsula that would allow all the prep work for a meal. Whether we were using a chopper to cut up celery or carrots (kid friendly of course) or stirring the bowl of mashed potatoes. It didn't matter how messy the counter became because it was their creation. My sons talked about their day and funny happenings at school or sometimes we would have serious talks all while preparing a meal or baking. They had their own bowl to add vegetables and spices. Mashed potatoes would take on a story—a cave, an igloo as they stirred and added broccoli. Those florets became trees to them in a snowy forest of adventure. They weren't thinking about the results but we enjoyed the process. Funny to think that their fraction sense increased without them even having math-phobia when the time came to learn about fractions.

Sweets were even more fun because they could eat the

toppings while mixing. Easy bake ovens weren't made to enable a child to make Pinterest perfect cakes. They were made to allow for imagination and play whatever the outcome, it was the process of each step. The smells filled the air and the sweetness rolled around their imaginations like a playground of pure joy. How can you explain the excitement of when the bell rings because the timer on the oven goes off? Whoever would think a timer would be so exciting? But it's not about the perfection of what will come out from that timer going off but the pure joy of accomplishment and a feeling of the process became their own creation. Their imperfection, happy, imaginative creation!

Whether a child is at school or at home, they will need to feel safe to explore creativity and not be judged or ridiculed for it. By focusing on the process, we allow our children to build a skill set that will follow them throughout their adult life. Patience and staying with the task is a life lesson we have to help our children acquire. For example, if we interfere with their "process" moments for the pure fact that we need to add our judgement or take over their creativity, then our children will abandon all reliance on their intuitions and fear the process instead of embracing it and celebrating it. Their independent thinking will be abandoned and replaced with looking to others for approval or having it done for them. The process in and of itself will bring joy if it holds value by the child and the family/friends that surround that child as they develop.

Without interference in the creative process or judgement, enjoying the process will unlock the creativity within ourselves and our children.

Enjoy the Process at Home

Home is the place where our children get to be free to play and imagine. The home is a place to dress up and pretend, taking on the role of characters and real life heroes like doctors, teachers, firefighters, and chefs, just to name a few. So it's important to have those items around the house. That might mean that you will have cardboard cutout plates around the kitchen or blocks in the bathtub. Or hit the stores after holidays, like Halloween, to buy clearance costumes for dress up and creativity all year long. Tremendous learning and development happens when children are left to create.

They don't need adult supervision when it comes to imaginative play. It is their story, their time, their commitment to attending to the play without judgement. It is so important to their social, emotional and cognitive growth. Research has shown us that these experiences lead to an improvement in memory, oral-language ability, and deep connection with literacy activities throughout their school years. If that's a car or spaceship that they built, then go along with it. Ask them where their spaceship is going? Who might they meet along the way? This play eventually matures into drawing and writing about the characters.

Does this sound familiar? All she wanted for her birthday was an easy bake oven. The little girl gets the toy and begins to mix and of course things can get a little messy. She is not aware of her surroundings and if she is even making a mess but she certainly is having a wonderful time creating a cake of her dreams. Her mother comes over and starts to raise her voice about the mess she is making and starts to clean up around her. After feeling bad, the mother then insists on playing along but starts to direct the play. "Maybe we should make these into cupcakes instead of a cake." "Look, you can put these cute little sprinkles on top and add this decoration."

This happens all too many times. I'm certain it happened in my house many times over with my boys. In order for children to create they need to tap into their hearts and imaginations without the adults taking over their creative vision.

Enjoying the Process at School

Where can our children find the magic outside of their homes? There has been much debate over the years about process vs. product learning in schools. We know that all children have different interests and they all learn differently. It is imperative for classrooms to find a balance where process driven work is a focus for learning new material before expectations can be placed on a child's mastery on an assessment. Whether it be a quiz, test or project, teachers need to focus on special learning outcome.

For example if you are testing a child's understanding of multiplication there might need to be different questions to reach all learners so they can show their understanding of multiplication whether it's drawing groups of equal amounts or using manipulatives etc. If a student continues to score low on tests it's so important for the teacher to dive deeper into the student's portfolio of work to see why the gaps exist. So looking closely at a child's pattern of learning, you will start to see information that can guide you to determining what is the best intervention and assistance that children would need to grow further academically, socially and emotionally. I know you're probably thinking what does social and emotion have to do with this.

These areas are just as important as academics. If a child is isolated during lunch and recess or during the day has difficulty working in groups with his peers, there needs to be clear steps—a process—by which you help that child understand the ways in which they can help themselves in situations. Children are not born knowing what to do; they have to be taught and spoken to many many times with care and love.

If your child mentions they are having difficulty at lunch there lies a perfect opportunity to discuss strategies to help them develop. You can have your child role play the problem and offer examples of what to say or do in that situation. Then switch roles and have them practice what to say or do. So that imaginative play that needed to happen when they were four years old will come in handy when they grow older and social pressures rears its head. Again role playing at 4 will be different than at 14 but having those skills are so important.

So there's been so much information about the value of

process driven in the classroom I'll teach you what happens in school and then guide you what to do at home:

Product Driven at School

◊ The teacher has given a sample for the students to replicate and copy.

◊ The student's finished piece of work looks the same as all the other student's work.

◊ There is a right and wrong way to proceed with the learning.

◊ The teacher will "fix mistakes" throughout the process to ensure that the end product is the same.

◊ The student might experience frustration and low self-esteem as he/she tries to fit their work into the vision of the teacher or class as a whole.

Product Driven at Home

◊ The parent interjects in a child's play.

◊ The parent will "fix mistakes" throughout the homework or project sometimes to the extent of writing it for them.

◊ The parent will do the report or project as the child sits quietly and watches.

◊ The child experiences frustration and low self-esteem.

◊ The child will not do the work or play on their own.

◊ The child will continually ask for help or be so passive that they will wait for their parent before jumping into the learning or making.

To understand a process driven classroom we could study the work of Dr. Scardamalia who has lit the educational world on fire with her research on Knowledge Building Principles. One principle talks about children taking responsibility for their own learning.

This process would include:

1. Setting goals.
2. Making choices.
3. Asking questions.
4. Choosing resources.
5. Making connections and seeing how we each learn so we could tap into the community resources.

This process driven way will lead to a product that the children will own. An end result that took many steps and skills to carry out with bumps and failures along the way. That is growth . . . that is learning—it's messy. Creativity has now been infused in classrooms.

How does this apply to creativity? Creativity is the process by which we allow our children, our students, to see their learning as independent. If we do not allow ourselves to be creative then we will never know the skills we have inside of us to bring to the learning table. How do I want to learn about this topic? Why is it important to me to do things this way? Children will be able to self-direct their learning. They will collaborate as well as work independently. But first they have to get to know who they are and how they learn. Once they know about themselves and their peers they will see a clear path to work together towards a learning goal.

Art has a way of showing us our creativity if we just allow it to happen. All art forms have to be an integral part of every content area and embedded into the curriculum. It cannot be detached from it as it gives children who can't otherwise understand the content an entry point into it. It will help children understand how they think and learn. Just to give you an example, if your child is learning fractions, it would be wonderful to use instruments or sticks to tap out the beat. ¼ note, ½ note. They even sell recorders (a type of flute) in the dollar stores around the country. You can tap out the note while your child plays the note. (One, two . . . breathe . . . three, four.)

If we look at an early childhood classroom, we should be able to see that the focus is not about the product but the process. Here are opportunities for teachers to let the creativity and higher order thinking skills come out. Learning through play and experimenting with different resources to bring about a learning situation. Can you imagine if the messages about creativity and learning were cut off at an early age. Here is what the research says:

According to the National Association for the Education of Young Children (NAEYC):

Process Art:

◊   There's no sample, pattern or model.
◊   Your child explores lots of interesting materials.

◊   Adults have no idea what children will create.

◊   There's no right or wrong way to do the art.

◊   Children are relaxed and focused.

◊   Your child wants to do more.

◊   The art is truly an "original" every time.

In addition, children react differently to product art vs. process art.

Children doing product art might say:

"Can I be done now?"

"Is this right?"

"Mine doesn't look right."

"I can't do this!"

Children doing process art might say:

"Can I have more time?"

"Can I have more paper?"

"Is there any yellow?"

"I want to make another one."

Allowing our children to focus on the process, we too have to allow their growth to happen. Do not be afraid to break down your child's misunderstanding and give them a means to say openly, I'm strong with understanding multiplication but I'm having difficulty when I get to multiplying 2 digit numbers.

Here are some conversation starters for inquiry based and process learning:

◊   What will happen if . . .?

◊   How did you . . .?

◊   How could we/you find that out . . .?

◊ What makes you say that?

◊ How do you know that?

◊ What do you want to find out?

◊ What are you wondering about?

Building confidence towards growth and process using this language:

◊ I noticed you didn't give up when you felt frustrated.

◊ I am proud of the risk you took today.

◊ I am so happy you kept trying today.

◊ Way to turn your mistake into an opportunity.

◊ I love the way you went back and improved your work.

◊ In our home we help each other grow and do our best.

If Your Child Says:	You Can Say or Have Them Say:
I don't understand.	What do you think you are missing?
This is too hard.	This may take some time.
I can't make this any better.	Is this really your (my) best work?
I am not good at this.	Add "yet" to the end of what you just said to me.
I can't read/do math.	You are going to train your brain to read/do math.

Try to catch yourself. Think about it! The next time your child wants to be creative, take a pause when you want to correct them; take a pause when you want to interject. Of course you might want to clear the calendar because so many times our children are deep into play and it's "Let's go," and we are off to our over-booked lives. For our children to be immersed into the process, they need time to be free to play and imagine.

Helping our children change their words will help them change their mindset and grow by leaps and bounds both academically, socially and emotionally.

CREATIVE CUES

Set of Steps

Everyone loves a set of steps to use because it takes the thinking out of the situation but let's say for a moment we use this concept to show our children that everyone's steps might be different to solve a problem.

Choose an activity that you and your child can do together. Everyone has the same supplies but the end result will be different because we all think and create differently. You can use Play-Doh, model magic, paints, or cut up paper, fabric, glue, tape, etc.

For example, if your child is having difficulty making friends, you can ask them to create a friend. As you're creating it will be the perfect opportunity to discuss friendship. You can tell stories about your friends that you grew up with. After you're done with the "making", discuss the steps they took to create it. Focusing on the steps will allow them to see clearly their creative spirit within. "I love how you decided to use the scraps to make . . ."

String Art

With a box of toothpicks and some Styrofoam and string you can help your child make beautiful string art with no directions . . . just the process. Place toothpicks around the Styrofoam in a circle, square, rectangle or really any shape you can think of. Once the toothpicks are pressed halfway to three quarters of the way in you can begin to wrap the string around the toothpicks and find another toothpick across the way or to the side and wrap around it.

Children continue to pick the toothpicks at random and will realize that some toothpicks or areas of the Styrofoam are missing and might need to be covered—or not—they use their imaginations. There is no right or wrong way for the finished product to look like.

Remember to post your creative work #GMBMCProcess

Everyday Items Bring Out Our Creativity

Set up a bin or cabinet to place all these everyday items. Children will start to see toilet paper rolls as columns to a building, yogurt cups as hats or small houses. What could you do with paint and toothbrushes?

Have your child experiment and get their creative juices going. Watercolor and a straw are great to help children see how they drip and bleed on the paper. What would happen if the paper is dry and you blow air through the straw? Does wet paper with watercolor paint do the same thing? How about using whisks and potato mashers as well as different sizes of brushes. Make lots of imprints and strokes using brushes, whisks. Why is it different? What does it look like?

CREATIVITY BREAK

Scrabble is a great way to get the mind thinking creatively.

Pick up 15 letters of your choice and try to make as many words using these pieces. Try to use those words to create a picture, piece of writing or a structure out of Legos or Play-Doh.

See where your creative mind takes you!

KEY #8

APPRECIATE YOUR LEARNING STYLE

One Size Does Not Fit All

*"Education begins the moment we see children as innately wise
and capable beings.
Only then can we play along in their world."*
~ Vince Gowmon

When shopping for clothing there is hardly ever a "one size fits all." Could you imagine if there was no variety when ordering food. We cannot expect our education system to treat all students the same when it comes to content and pedagogy.

We are all different in so many beautiful and wonderful ways. We grow and learn at different rates. Children come to school with different learning experiences which put demands on schools and teachers to try to "fit them" into a classroom that matches their ability. It is important for me to spend some time in this chapter discussing the role schools take today to ensure there is attention given to the individual student.

Schools in the 19th and 20th century were made to mimic the structure of manufacturing systems. Teachers had the "front" of a room with a chalk board and the students sat in rows and columns with a task to be quiet and absorb, memorize and recite back what was taught. There was little time spent conferencing with students and asking in depth questions.

Through the years along with extensive research we start to see a change in our understanding of how students think. Convergent thinking, the ability to arrive at a single correct answer was the norm for many many years and sometimes we see some glimpses even today with traditional pedagogy coming from seasoned teachers.

Today because of the work of Howard Gardner, he has helped us to see through research that children have multiple intelligences. He helped us see that learning goes beyond a linear way of thinking. It is very divergent in its nature. Divergent thinking helps the child to see that there could be multiple answers and this way of thinking is essential to creativity.

Years ago classrooms followed a curriculum that was taught through a set of workbooks and a teacher's guide helped the teacher know what to do before, during and after each lesson. Even what to say. Today, curriculum has been divided by content areas that exist with a set of standards that guide the school districts to help their students understand essential questions and overarching themes. School districts spend countless hours connecting curriculum to lessons and guiding teachers to refer to resources that will support it.

Today classrooms are changing in that teachers explain the lesson objective and even model an example or set of steps needed to understand the algorithm or assignment. Students go off to practice the learning and the teacher will then strive to gather a few students to work on their appropriate skill or strategy needed to advance their learning. Small group instruction, centers, and differentiation are used to meet the needs of different learners. Pacing schedules and testing often take over the pulse and rhythm of the days. Deadlines to meet for standardized testing and work to cover so the student is ready for a possible question on these rigorous tests causes much stress and anxiety not only for the teacher but the student.

Where can creativity fit in?

Creativity has been challenged because the mindset is that it is driven as an artistic endeavor. Creativity starts with a type of thinking. It then is supported by research and exemplars that bring that thinking to life. If children create alone they will see that tremendous benefit is experienced when they share their ideas and collaborate with others. They can then reformulate their ideas and try out their thinking. Creativity flourishes when you find others who share your vision and passion as I referred to in previous chapters. Let me share a story of how creativity changed one of my student's lives.

Years ago, when I was a 5th grade teacher in a suburban school district, I had a student who didn't feel confident as a writer. He refused to spend time with his thoughts or trust his voice within himself. As in all the years of my teaching I would spend September and October getting to know my students. I would give them a questionnaire as well as their parents and I would try to find out "how" they learned. What was their learning style? I would also find out what they enjoyed doing outside of school—their interests and their passions.

This one student who had difficulty with writing loved Harry Potter. His backpack, pencil cases, clothing all had some type of Harry Potter reference. He could rattle off every detail of every character. He could describe the buildings and the settings of each story.

Our genre for the marking period was Informational Writing. Usually teachers would encourage their students to dive into Non-fiction research in the hope that they would learn factual information and increase their student's vocabulary by immersing them in a concentrated reading of that subject area. My students were researching events like the Titanic and animal habitats just to name a few.

Would it be wrong to have this student write about the information he learned about Harry Potter's character and the structure of the settings throughout the different books?.

Can he inform the class to the extent that they could draw a map of the world of Harry Potter?

When I sat him down to conference I presented the idea to him and he was thrilled. Suddenly his fear of writing washed away and was replaced by his passion for the subject he was writing about. As we worked through the process of writing, coming up with a structure and idea for the piece, his imagination and creativity grew. He gathered his thoughts and used tremendous detail to inform us of the world he was reading about and came to love.

In writing classes around the world, students are given directions to complete a published piece on loose-leaf paper or some fancy stationery. Some students are encouraged to type their stories on a Word doc and print it out only to decorate a finished cover to be hung on a bulletin board. My class was the exception. Since we were all different, we had a class meeting about what our published pieces would look like. Student's imaginations were running wild with thoughts of building a paper titanic ship where the windows and port holes could open and display their written paragraphs.

As I scanned the room of excited students there stood my Harry Potter student once again in a state of defeat. He couldn't think of what to do to showcase his written work. He was overwhelmed by thoughts of drawing a map or how it might look if he tried to draw. His confidence in art was low.

"I can't do this," he explained in the saddest sound a voice could make.

I started to question him about Harry Potter and his character traits. Focusing him on describing the physical features. I asked him if he knew what register tape looked like? He realized it was in my writing center. He ran over to grab it and said what does this have to do with Harry Potter? Can you write your story on this paper as a type of scroll? The creative light went on. What better way to understand and explain about the world of Harry Potter than to have the writing come through the scar.

The plan was in place. Find a life-size head of Harry Potter and trace it. Embellish it with crayons, markers, string and other art materials. The student carefully and diligently wrote his informational text onto the register tape. When the author's celebration was about to begin the students were in awe at how he read his writing and slowly pulled it through Harry Potter's scar. Inspiration and this experience not only led to the student's growth in creativity but everyone else's.

How can we meet the needs of our children in and outside of the classroom? Creativity! Giving our children opportunities to learn in ways that meet them where they are at. For example, if I gave the same reading assignment to all students it would be equal but it wouldn't serve all the students who needed extra help because they struggle as readers. On the other hand, some students need more complicated texts to grow their reading ability.

Let's compare this thinking to medicine. You wouldn't give the same prescription to someone who has an allergy or who has different symptoms that require a different medication. You would treat the patient for their individual needs based on their symptoms or how they present themselves at the time of their examination. It's the same situation with our children. If a child is coming to school every day and presenting with difficulties then the teacher and family needs to address their needs so the child can grow and thrive.

Did you ever shop for plants that you would like to place inside or outside of your home? Each plant comes with a precise tag stuck in the dirt that reads the exact environment or food/water schedule needed for it to thrive and grow. In fact you would never treat a cactus and an orchid the same way. Each plant needs its own specific growing environment. Would they both grow if we gave them the same resources? We cannot think that the same prescription would work for everyone in the classroom and at home. We are all different, unique and special in our own way.

Over the years as an educator I have seen many students lose their way because their needs were not taken into account. Today we have differentiation and other strategies that meet the child where they're at. Here are some strategies:

1. Ask your child what they are interested in learning about and keep a chart for each subject.

2. Keep a close eye on your child when they are learning something new. What supports do they need to be successful?

3. Help your child understand difficult content by finding out how best they learn from the presentation of material. (i.e., video, audio, visual, hardcopy)

4. Use the Learning Style checklist in Chapter 2 to find out what kind of intelligence your child has which would help you to know what kind of learning environment they need to grow.

5. Does his/her teacher teach to the whole class or are there opportunities for small group instruction, individualized learning, stations or centers?

Using the learning style chart can be an eye opener for children and their families. But what do you do once you find out how your child learns? Make them aware of the learning style and remind them that everyone is different and unique. We all approach learning in a different way and our brains respond to what style comes easiest for us. That doesn't mean we don't expose our children to other learning styles. We need to keep an open mind so our children can grow, they might even change learning styles throughout their life. Start with what they're comfortable with to help them build confidence and then go from there.

Here are just a few ideas to support each learning style and unlock the creative child within:

NOTE- BOX

Visual/Spatial
◊ Create a map
◊ Paint a picture
◊ Make a sculpture
◊ Drawing nature/draw anything
◊ Murals

◊ Make a mobile with string, paper and a wire clothes hanger

◊ Collage scraps of paper, metal, wood and anything from the recycling bin

◊ Cartoons

◊ Ads

◊ 3D drawings

◊ Make a storyboard

◊ Mosaics made from paper or tile

◊ Posters

Verbal/Linguistic

◊ Books to read

◊ Journals/diary to write in

◊ Humor/jokes

◊ Storytelling

◊ Solve word puzzles

◊ Interview a family member

◊ Listening (books on tape)

Naturalist

◊ Collect rocks, leaves or anything in nature

◊ Take out field guides from the library and go on a nature walk

◊ Observe birds

◊ Fish

◊ Gardening: plant seeds, flowers, vegetables

◊ Keep track of the weather (chart and try to forecast)

◊ Star gazing

◊ Categorize rocks

◊ Observe habitats

Interpersonal Intelligence

◊ Person to person communication

◊ Practice empathy

◊ Group projects

◊ Games

◊ Campaign speeches

◊ Interviews

◊ Create a sales pitch for something you're passionate about

◊ Debate

◊ Give feedback

Logical/Mathematical

◊ Create formulas to solve problems

◊ Use graphic organizers to learn new material

◊ Create a timeline

◊ Create a spreadsheet

◊ Create a puzzle

◊ Calculate the tip at a restaurant

◊ Look for patterns around you

◊ Read *Grandfather Tang's Story* and take pieces of a Tangram and make different animals

Bodily Kinesthetic

◊ Dance around the house

◊ Play a sport

◊ Put on a skit for your family and friends

◊ Play charades

◊ Pantomime

◊ Any type of exercise

◊ Create a safe obstacle course in your backyard or home

◊ Create body language poses and guess what someone is feeling

Musical Rhythmic

◊ Play an instrument

◊ Tap out a melody

◊ Write a song

◊ Sing a song

◊ Join a choir

◊ Hum a tune

◊ Listen for sounds around you

◊ Take part in a musical performance

Intrapersonal

◊ Journaling

◊ Meditations

◊ Affirmations

◊ Guided imagery

◊ Autobiography

◊ Monologue

◊ Outline your body onto paper and put words and pictures about what you are thinking on your head, feeling on your heart . . .

◊ Think about your Thinking—Metacognition

◊ Reflection pages in your journal

These simple activities can be used at home or in school to help your child gain the confidence they need and attach anything they are learning so they can retain the information. Once you know how you or your child learns or enjoys life, you can easily adapt any situation at home or at school by meeting them where they are most comfortable. If they are at school and the learning environment does not support their learning style be sure to have these activities once they get home. For example, if your child is musical they can certainly tap out a beat and break down fractions by explaining it and attaching it to music. My boys loved the Rap Multiplication songs growing up.

When you help your child appreciate their learning styles and respect other learning styles they can feel free to think creatively. They will be able to adapt and problem solve any issue that comes their way. Even tackling the most difficult school work. Try it out!

CREATIVE CUES

Let's approach the Creative Cues in a different way in this chapter. Because we are talking about one size doesn't fit all then my Creative Cues would have to be activities that can be adaptable and altered to meet the needs of your child. The column to the right is a way for you to change it depending on your child's individual interests or learning style. Let's go!

Activity	Materials	Adaptations
Building Sculptures Children love to build as early as a toddler all the way up to high school	Wood blocks Legos Clay	Cardboard Toilet Paper and Paper towel roll tubes cut up Toothpicks and mini-marshmallows Pizza Dough Cookie Dough
Painting In any kind of weather, painting is a wonderful experience for all ages	Watercolors Brushes Acrylic Chalk	Spray-Painting with spray bottles Finger Painting Use trucks, cars, etc. to see if the wheels can make a print or texture on the paper Instead of brushes, use different types of leaves

Collage Children are amazed to see things overlap and come together	Paper Stickers Photos Glue	Draw a shape then fill it with the materials listed. It can be a letter, number, animal or object Combining textures, fabrics, and using mixed media Cut, rip, sew, tear, fold, tuck can make it become 3D.
Mobiles Objects suspended in air by a string or wire make children's imaginations come to life	String Paper Cardboard Wire	Mobiles can represent a story map of characters and setting on cards with detail information about plot on the backside. What if children build a mobile to show their understanding of the life cycles in science or simple shapes and colors for younger children?

Any of these activities can be combined with a subject area to represent a child's understanding of the concepts. Building structures can incorporate shapes, lines and simple geometric concepts. This is just a snapshot of creative activities to begin with when we need to bring out our children's creativity.

CREATIVITY BREAK

Make a Stuffy Fluffy

1. Draw a large face or character on paper.
2. Use that paper as a template.
3. Lay the sweater flat on a table making sure front and back are together and flattened out.
4. Place the template on the sweater and pin catching the front and back of sweater.
5. Cut around your template making sure you are cutting through the front and back of sweater.
6. Remove paper.
7. Add eyes, nose and mouth using other fabric (felt, etc.) to the top piece only. Remember when you are sewing the eyes, nose, mouth you are only sewing it to the top piece only.
8. After decorating and embellishing it, lay the top piece back onto the back of the sweater and sew around the edges leaving a small opening.
9. Place polyester fill inside the small opening until you decide your desired "fluffiness"
10. Close up the small opening with thread.
11. Hug and cherish forever.

KEY #9

NOTICE EVERY DETAIL

Can't We Just Look Up?

"Knowledge comes from looking around, Wisdom comes from looking up."
~ Adrian Rogers

As a kid I experienced a field trip that would take me on a creative journey throughout my life. I was a 7th grader on a bus into Manhattan to see the King Tut exhibit with my art class. In the 70's class trips into the city was normal and very exciting. We had our tickets and we went to the Metropolitan Museum of Art. As our class was exiting off the bus, "Look up" my teacher would say and we took in the enormous building that stood before us. The building that would resonate as a happy place, a place to go to lift your soul, a place that would bring to life the creativity that was longing to get out.

As we entered into a small gallery that would lead us to the exhibit, my teacher called us together to talk about the artwork that was around us. We slowly took in every painting and drawing as if to find ourselves in it or connect us to go back in time to understand what the artist and the world was going through. I found myself breathing in its spectacular colors and shapes and figures. Suddenly the class was sitting on the floor. No, it was directed for us to, "lie on the floor."

Was my teacher going mad? Did she know we were middle school kids aware of what our friends would say or how we would look?

A couple of brave kids led the way and we all followed. The cold floor relaxed us and we started to see the beautiful architectural ceiling that was filled with patterns, color, paintings and we didn't want to get up. Looking up had a new meaning. Could I be lost in that space above? Could I remove myself from the noise of the crowds and school chatter of other classes and be present in the midst of beauty? Why wasn't anyone noticing what we noticed? What could be so important than to take a moment to "look up?" My teacher helped me to see beyond what was in front of me. To help my imagination grow and making me conscious of the space around me. My world was changed forever.

"Up"

The word "up" can imply so many things. As a kid your mom would say, "sit up" or "stand up straight, no slouchers here." After a loss in a sporting game, "Keep your chin up, there's always next time." Up can mean winning. The Yankees are "Up" 3-0 in the bottom of the 7th inning. But up to me meant taking the time to look above in all things. Taking time to notice the roof line, the sky or maybe the top of a tree. Look up meant looking forward to wonderful things that will come.

Noticing the details in life helps our mind and brain to think of things in a different way, therefore resulting in new ideas or thoughts. Just changing the environment can work wonders for your creativity. A park, a hike, or sitting at the beach in the off season can help—the sounds are different. Have you ever just noticed the different sounds around you?

I remember meeting a poet who explained that in order to write poetry he would sit for hours and observe the object he was writing about. So for example, if he wanted to write about a train. He would visit train museums or train stations and write everything he noticed in his notebook. Details: see, hear, smell, emotion, actions of the train and the riders

Noticing the details brings our creativity to a deeper level. If you need to be more creative, change your environment and take in all the beauty and details of life.

When my boys were young, I would take them to museums or any structure inside or outside and help them to "Look up." I did lie on the floor of the museum to let them know it was okay to do this and see the perspective. Capturing that moment was a gift to be treasured. We are all fascinated when we go to a museum or any building when we sight see on vacations.

During my years of teaching I had an opportunity to take school kids on an Architectural tour of St. George. Right off the ferry terminal on the Staten Island side lies government buildings, shops and homes that dated back to the early 1900's to buildings representing different architectural features. With clipboards in each student's hands, they had to use the guide to search out these features during the walking tour. The neighborhood looked different to them after that session. But the learning didn't happen until they went back into their classroom. They had to use the knowledge that was learned to create their own structure and identify the different architectural features in it.

This dive into architecture helps students see the beauty around them and appreciate art in a structure. Once again creativity rears its head. Transforming their lives and helping them to notice. The classroom was buzzing with discussions about what kind of structure they would build. First they drew the designs in their notebooks and for those who were adventurous they went to the supply corner and grabbed a larger piece of paper. They started to imagine their building and what it would be used for. Some children imagined a dome shaped school building where tunnels helped the flow from one domed area to another. Other children wanted their buildings to be tall and stately.

The class decided on materials and brought in the supplies on a designated day. There was Styrofoam, cardboard, straws, balsam wood, fabric, construction paper, wide and narrow popsicle sticks, cereal boxes, tissue boxes, clear lids from milkshakes and yogurt cups. Without instructions students were able to build their vision in 3D. It took a little over a week and their work grew into a gallery display for all to see. I truly believe that as they were building, they fell into a type of zone where nothing or no one was going to distract them. They were focused and determined to build. Anyone watching or passing by the classroom saw the internal joy of making, building, creating and sharing their ideas with their classmates. It was pure joy to watch their happiness expand with each day.

Field Trip Thoughts

That poet I met years ago would be amazed if he met my class—amazed at the way they looked at every detail of the birds they were watching at the birdfeeder; amazed at the way they could take those details and grab their writer's notebook to record their findings, their observations. They noticed everything—the feeder and the way the birds would peck and grab their food. When they researched their own bird that they chose to investigate, they would excitedly show me how the pictures they would find about the type of egg the bird would lay, or perhaps the nest. Each different and unique in their own way. "Like each one of us," I would explain. "We are all different and we live in different houses but we are all special." How I wanted my words to wrap them like a quilted blanket of hope. Day after day we would recognize the similarities and differences. We were getting ready to share in our joy of birdwatching with an expert. My students couldn't get enough.

We ventured out once a week to fill the birdfeeder outside the classroom. It didn't matter the weather, they would remind me, "We have to feed the birds." Can I have a turn today? They were 2nd graders and becoming more responsible with each passing day. This project was instilling life skills into them and I was filled with joy to watch their progress and growth. Caring human beings out to change the world. To be part of a feeder-watch effort to help scientists keep track of migration and changes. My students saw themselves as part of a bigger world and not just a classroom in a small town.

They wanted to share their findings with the school and we decided as a class to create a digital story book. The book was comprised of photographs. Photographs they would find about their bird and photos we would take. Yes, photographs do motivate children to write. Their visual world became a canvas to create informational pieces of writing. They knew their audience and for writers that is one of the most important things. They wanted their families and friends to know specific facts and details. It wasn't time for fantasy or narrative writing, it was fact finding and captions and charts. It was pure, raw details. They wanted these amazing findings of their research to be communicated. They did just that! *All about Birds* was written by my Second Graders and could still be found in that school's library, catalogued and checked out. Parents were happy to buy bird food and even some bought binoculars. The joy of seeing details up close. The joy of investigating and the curiosity of their children made them want to join in the learning. So many beautiful moments were made on that day. Bagged lunches, binoculars and birds.

As the students traveled alongside Sam, they skipped through the fields. When Sam would stop and point out a Robin's nest, they would stop and listen closely and then off they went again throughout the trail.

How to Notice Details at Home

Start with Nature: Field trips are an amazing way to get out for the day and emerge yourself in the wonders that are around us. So many county and state parks offer a tremendous amount of programs to connect children and adults to nature. Don't forget to bring along a field guide. Maybe you want to dive into finding out more about trees or insects? Take along the guide to take their learning and observation skills to a new level. Of course you can take pictures and have them printed to be glued into a writing notebook/journal. Sometimes we need to sit a while with a photograph. Ask your child, "What's going on in this photograph?" What details do you see that makes you say that? I always love the prompt, "I wonder . . ."

Details help us:
◊   to communicate with one another
◊   give us an invitation to see beyond the surface
◊   to dive deeper into meaning
◊   make an emotional connection or reaction

◊   become engaged with the world around us instead of passively walking through life

How To Notice Details At School

Notice the details in your textbooks or the classroom library books you take out. Ask, "Did I learn something new? What did I notice that was unexpected?" In the classroom and outside the school there are so many wonderful details happening. What's different today that I didn't notice yesterday? Find one thing that's different today in your school? Are the trees/shrubs budding? Has the color of the grass or sky changed? Why? The examples of limitless.

Is writing an art form? I'll let you be the judge of that . . .

Writing and Meditation

During my participation at a Slow Fashion Retreat in Bar Harbor Maine, we were asked to bring our making to a mediation and writing session with Katherine Ferrier. She gathered us at a table on the porch overlooking the coast and instructed us to agree to show up and to attend to. It's amazing what a willingness "to attend" and "to stay" can do for creativity. I immediately dove into the experience of taking in the beautiful Bar Harbor landscape as we picked up our making (knitting, hand stitching, coloring, etc.). After a while, we then were instructed to put down our making and write about what we noticed. My head exploded with observations of the cool summer breeze, birds chirping, sailboats waiting for its owner, my journey of connectivity, a reunion of stories and soul searching adventures. My hand couldn't write fast enough.

We were directed to stop and pick up our making again while Katherine quoted Natalie Goldberg and asked us to play with meaning and metaphor. Back to writing again, but this time we were asked to attend to what gnaws at us. Part of an artist's life is a lifetime work of uncovering 1-2 things that gnaw at them. What draws our attention?

"The more space you make in yourself to listen and receive . . ." Katherine continued.

I love to see . . . The writing continued with deep breaths, and I listened and received these thoughts. *I love to see my boys laughing and enjoying their time together as brothers . . . I love to see waves crash upon the shore in different rhythms, pulling in sand and rock . . . People hold their breath and dive in. How can something so powerful be so beautiful at the same time.*

Katherine pulled out of all of us some of the most interesting thoughts that lay buried and yet when they surfaced had so much meaning connected to them. Metaphor and meaning. "You can begin anywhere, add a little something, like improv Jazz music. Spirit of being willing to be surprised."

When we analyzed our writing and picked 2-3 phrases that jumped out at us. We continued with our making, but this time Katherine continued to help us meditate some more. "But whatever our motivation may be . . . to become more of whom we'd like to be and who we would like to become . . . underlying intent is self-transformation."

She read a beautiful poem by Marge Percy "To Be of Use" and we all continued to "make." We then stopped and added to the previous writing by using the same prompt: "I see. I notice. I hear." This time we had to add, "This reminds me of..."

My writing continued. *I see the anchored sailboats anchored and silent... This reminds me that life is too short to never find time to enjoy the things you love. I notice the birds chirping. This reminds me of the home I left behind where my birdfeeders were always happily occupied.*

This writing meditation brought out some underlying thoughts that probably would've stayed hidden. We rewrote all the phrases that jumped out of the paper and added them to the others. Finally we repeated one phrase three times and the magic came out of the exercise. Katherine helped us dive in and reach out to grab hold of the underlying intent. I have continued to close each of my meditation and writing rituals by practicing what Katherine taught us... breathe in what's hurt in the world and breathe out PEACE! Thank you Katherine Ferrier for giving us a wonderful base in which to practice. She truly is a Zen master!

The poem was finished. Raw and full of my noticing. Here's my poem:

Enjoy the Things You Love

Enjoy the things you love
Songbirds whistling begging us
to be part of their beautiful world

Picnics in the park
Bird feeders that were happily
occupied
Enjoy the things you love
Waves crash and birds dive
into the powerful chaos
Different movements and rhythms
remind us of our uniqueness
Cleansing us
until we are smooth
Enjoy the things you love

Looking up from our phones, from our routines and taking in what's around and noticing can bring enlightenment about yourself. Noticing and being present enough to grab the beauty, joy and surprise. Give yourself that beautiful space in which to make the magic inside of you come out.

"We travel because we need to, because distance and difference
are the secret topic of creativity. When we get home, home is still
the same.
But something in our mind has been changed and that changes
everything.
~ Jonah Lehrer

I was forever changed by my trip to Bar Harbor, Maine.

CREATIVE CUES

Look up and Notice

Take time to look up at the sky and notice maybe clouds or birds. Try to breathe and let your imagination take over. Do you start to see pictures in the clouds or maybe a pattern of birds in flight? Observe and watch the movement. You can sketch, paint or write about those clouds and birds too or anything that you notice.

Take Note of Buildings

What do you notice about the tops of the structures of the buildings? How are they the same? Different? There are many ways to study buildings. Grab a blank sheet of paper and jot down some of your favorite architectural design. Where have you seen them before? You can also enlarge the pictures and make playing cards during a family drive into a local city or town. See how many features you can find.

Meditation and Prayer

"No one speaks to God these days," lyrics from A Star is Born. I remember hearing those words sung in that movie and thinking about my own spirituality. It can bring tremendous peace to meditate on all of the blessings in your life. Capturing the positivity each day in a meditation or art activity. So many times we realize that when our lives slow down a bit we can think clearly and find time to rejoice in the blessings in our lives and those around us.

Observe and Remember

Connect what you observe to a memory or experience you've had in the past (i.e. I notice or I see and This reminds me of . . .) Reflective writing allows us to dig in deep and connect our present with our past. Our hearts and minds see that new experience combined with our prior knowledge to bring us into a new dimension of growth and understanding. Seeing through a new set of eyes.

"It's not what life throws at us that determine what our life will be now, so much as how much of ourselves we're willing to throw into life."
~ Author Unknown

CREATIVITY BREAK

Take the first letter of your name, and write 10-15 descriptive words that begin with that letter and describe you! Design an Alphabet Square and draw pictures that go with the letter and your name. Do this together with your child for even more fun!

KEY #10

CREATE PRECIOUS MOMENTS

They'll Last A Lifetime

"The best thing to spend on your children is time."
~ Louise Hart

Sometimes precious moments are unplanned.

It was the middle of the winter and the days felt like they went on forever. I left for work in the morning. My older son was dropped off at a before school program by his dad each day. The elementary school would feed them breakfast and he would spend every morning in a school building waiting for his day to start with other kids just like him. His dad would commute into New York City and I would take my younger son to a daycare close to the school where I taught. My son would quietly eat his cheerios and drink his juice box. Not much of a breakfast selection when you have two working parents and both of them commute over

40 min each way to work. We always made the best out of it by telling stories, talking about sports, family events to look forward to or just singing songs off a CD.

Trying to create some precious moments even in the car. The routine after work would be to pick both boys up from school and head home to cook dinner and start our night routines of homework, dinner, down time and bedtime. This cold winter day we were all bundled to face the extreme temperatures and the wind blowing in our faces so forcefully we gasped for breath as our breath escaped into the cold. That short distance from the school to the car felt like we were climbing Mt. Everest.

My day was mentally exhausting from giving my everything to the students in my classroom. My body was tired from staying up late to grade papers and worrying if my own boys were learning and growing at school. The laundry was piling up, bills had to be paid and there always seemed to be dishes to wash or emptied from the dishwasher. I just wanted to get home from work, grab a blanket and some tea and curl up on the couch to rest. If you know anything about me, I never take naps, but today could have been one of those days.

When the boys and I arrived home, I dropped all tote bags, book bags, lunch boxes and mail to the floor and removed jackets, boots and shoes. Just a moment to catch my breath, a moment of peace, of relaxation . . .

My boys went right to the couch and started jumping and somehow the pillows were coming off. "Mom, let's build a fort!"

This is not the time. Pick another day, I thought. But the look in their sweet eyes pulled my heartstrings.

Slowly, I got up and sat on the floor by the couch. I would need blankets and sheets to make this work. My older son had a plan and was happy to share the plans out loud. He knew exactly how the walls would be made from the larger cushions and the smaller ones to barricade the sides. My younger son who was only two years old at the time was running around in a circle. He knew something exciting was coming. We grabbed flashlights and toys that matched the imaginative land we were creating. Slowly my energy returned and my heart jumped for joy to watch my sons involved in this creative play. Their imaginations made a fort that protected us from the tigers and bears in the forest.

"Shhhh, Mommy, do you hear them roaring?"

We all got in a huddle, squatting down, my younger son's finger on his lips and lights were off! The winter moonlight was coming through the townhouse window but the glow of our hearts and minds made the winter blustery day dissolve away.

I didn't see it coming—the precious moment morphed out of a dark, dreary winter day because I allowed the light of this creative idea to make its way into our lives. We agreed to be present in the moment when all life obligations and selfish feelings were put to the side to have a chance to let this fort take shape. Flashlights, stuffed animals, action figures, and of course a book to read—*Brown Bear, Brown Bear What Do You See?*

After dinner that night we returned to the fort and played some more. Somehow that night they slept soundly and the hugs seemed deeper and longer. Yes, that's what precious moments do, they touch your heart and soul in such a way that they will live on forever in your mind. Sheets, towels, blankets, dish towels, even when the roof would collapse we would find a way to hold it up—maybe with a broomstick in the middle or tie the corners of the sheet to the bannister or to another sheet—the building, constructing, creating a place that took on a life of its own and I'm sure continued in my children's dream that night.

Creating Time

I love a good quote. But sometimes good quotes go underutilized. I'm sure you've heard phrases like this:

"Time is what we want most, but . . . what we use worst."

"Time is a cruel thief to rob us of our former selves. WE lose as much to life as we do to death."

"Time flies when you're having fun."

"We must use time as a tool, not as a crutch."

"If we take care of the moments, the years will take care of themselves."

"Lost time is never found again."

"Yesterday's the past, tomorrow's the future, but today is a gift. That's why it's called the present."

"Time flies over us, but leaves its shadow behind."

"Time is a created thing. To say, 'I don't have time,' is like saying, 'I don't want to.'"

"Time takes it all whether you want it to or not."

"Better three hours too soon than one minute too late."

"Time is the wisest counselor of all."

"Time is the school in which we learn, time is the fire in which we burn."

"Nothing is a waste of time if you use the experience wisely."

I know I've heard them, I've probably even said most if not all of them. But with all the hustle and bustle, never actually having time to take these phrases too seriously. Life keeps us moving. Life pushes and pulls us through a journey of emotional situations, balancing family activities and work schedules. There might be days when the car doesn't start or the appliance breaks down, days when the unexpected derails us. We push through and resolve issues only to have more put upon us. If we are blessed to have children in our lives, time really starts to pick up speed.

According to the Merriam-Webster dictionary *precious* means, "of great value; highly esteemed or cherished."

I do believe we could place objects as being precious but no amount of money can buy more time; it cannot buy moments we spend with our families. In a world that seems to move at a lightning fast speed these days it is more important than ever to slow down and give these precious moments a place in our lives.

In 2015, the Journal of Marriage and Family found that the amount of time parents spend with their kids ranging in ages of 3 to 11 had no significant relationship to how children will develop in the areas of academics, emotional intelligence and behavior. However, several studies did show that sharing precious moments such as engaging with their children, talking with them or reading to their children created positive outcomes. So it is not about the amount of time you spend but rather the quality of the time you spend with your children.

Often being in the same space together is not enough—it seems that everywhere you turn families are glued to screens or devices such as smart phones, iPads, and gaming systems. Thomas Kersting's book *Disconnected* shows a tremendous amount of research in linking children's technology use to "disconnectedness" in family, school and friends because of technology—it really is alarming. Increases in anxiety and lack of coping skills are leaving many children fearful of trusting their own intuition and tapping into their creativity.

Freezing Moments

Time doesn't stand still for anyone or anything. As a mother, I sometimes sit and wonder how 27 years could have passed by so quickly. I feel like I was just at a little league game or laughing together with my boys as we built forts in the living room on a rainy day.

We can freeze time by recalling a memory or looking at old photos and remembering what used to be. Scrapbooks became an obsession for me. I remember buying the paper, stickers, and embellishing pages to celebrate these moments of time. Maybe if I kept an account of those memories I can freeze time, I can keep these moments forever in case I wouldn't be able to remember them one day. If I get sad I can just look back and jump into those photos and hear the laughter of vacations, the excitement of bases loaded in the bottom of the 7th, and even the calmness and snuggles of a sleeping child in my arms. I guess pictures are worth a thousand words.

Every year as a teacher greeting my new students for the school year, I would wonder about my own children. I missed all the first days of school; putting them on the bus; waving goodbye; field trips; Halloween parades; last days of school; not being the first one they see as they run home to celebrate summer. It's not like I missed their nightly band concerts or plays. I could attend those. Anything after school or at night I was there. My working mom guilt would volunteer to bring in anything food related just to be a part of the daily routines of the school. If I couldn't be there to sell the cupcakes or school store stuff, then maybe I could donate, bake, etc. to feel like I was there spiritually. As a parent we just want to be there for everything.

My career and service to my community was where time had put me, to greet other families, securing them in knowing that everything will be okay. Riding on a bus for the many school trips I had to go on to celebrate learning with families. Then my mind would travel to thinking about my boys and how they were not there.

My heart ached but no one was able to see. You get really good at hiding your feelings when you're a teacher. You can't let anyone know, not the students, not the staff, and never the principal. You had to be strong, to be a role model, to be a keeper of everyone else's emotions, fears, and celebrations.

Each day when I picked up my boys from a program the school provided for working parents, I would see their faces. Some days the look would be, "What took you so long to get here?" or on other days, "I was just in the middle of finishing a game with my friend." Too early or too late I was there with open arms and a heart filled with love. Love them up even when they poured their day's happenings into the car ride home. As we drove home it was lots of conversations about what happened at school or at lunch but on those days when the car was really quiet, I knew something emotional happened. It took some time to get the conversation going and help them open up.

Hurt can do that, retreating and closing up can be the quickest mechanism to push away, push down and bury the days hurt, but soon enough you realize it's not the best decision. Those issues won't resolve themselves on their own. They have to be opened up like an artichoke. The hard pointy outside protects the soft beautiful heart inside. I can take in THEIR emotions, fears and celebrations of the school day. I can wrap my words and love around them to try to solve it and make it all better. I tried. Sometimes it worked and other times they just had to go through time to sort it out. I kept the conversation and words flowing even if they weren't ready to hear it or solve it.

Summers were spent playing catch up for the time I

lost with them during the school year. Carefully I planned events and experiences that would be memorable. Before school ended, I would spend hours on my lunch and prep time to start looking for summer activities. Museum visits would always be on the list. I would plan the summers like they were my lesson plans of life. Beach visits, ball games, picnics, creative play with paint, clay, and props. Saving large and small cardboard boxes came in handy. We made castles out of those large cardboard boxes. Wrapping aluminum foil around cut up pieces because every knight needs to protect his castle. We covered the cardboard shield with construction paper and drew symbols of our imaginative land. My love of sewing came into play and I stitched together old pieces of fabric to make capes. Somehow each summer became a theme.

We looked through newspapers and magazines to see if exhibits matched our adventure. We spent time in the library pulling books that would relate to that theme. DK Publishing had the best large hardcover nonfiction books on any topic. My boys loved visiting the dinosaur exhibit at the Museum of Natural History. Their plastic dinosaurs were now in front of them in real size. How we looked at them in wonderment. The size of those giants engulfed our minds and their imaginations grew even bigger.

Lighthouses were a big hit with my older son. We would search for them in books and on maps and then try to visit as many as we could. Field guides became our best friends. It's amazing what pictures can do for children. Some of the text in the books were over their heads, but it didn't matter, we could match the picture to what we were seeing and I would read the fancy names. They loved carrying them around and trying to match what they were seeing to what was in the book. If we went to the beach, the field guide on seashells came with us. If we took a walk in a state or county park, the plants and tree field guides came with us.

One summer we journaled everything. I guess we were practicing bullet journaling without even knowing it. Reading and writing were one in the summer. The experiences were magical and my boys bonded. Those lost hours and times I would worry about throughout the school year dissipated and I felt whole again . . . until another school year reared its head and I would be back to the crazy routines of taking care of a home, children, and a marriage.

Time doesn't stand still . . . It moves furiously and without notice your children are grown up. When I reflect now I think to myself, "I was always packing something." Packing a diaper bag, packing a lunch to put in a backpack, packing up their cleats and gloves for a baseball or basketball tournament. You go from packing all their childhood supplies to pack for college living in dorms. It doesn't stop there. You celebrate their graduations and then pack them up and help them set up their apartments for their independent life without you.

Routines, schedules and just pure life decisions have a way of pulling us away from the quiet still times that need to happen so families can have memories to last a lifetime when they're all grown up. "Time flies when you're having fun."

My Students Were My Mirror

Today as an administrator of an elementary school, I get to see the world of teaching and family dynamics in a different way. The whole school picture, the needs of families and teachers surfaces daily and like every situation we solve it differently for every different situation. Over the years I have had teachers send down students to the office because they couldn't seem to get them to do their work or focus. I remember there was this one time a third grade boy kept misbehaving and almost every day was in my office. We would discuss what happened in class. We would try to get to the bottom of why he was misbehaving or not doing his work. It was always something that could easily be solved but yet he didn't want to do what was asked of him in class. Finally after several months of repeated episodes, he broke down crying asking to see his mom. He was missing her and wanted to spend time with her. All I remember were phrases that kept coming out of his mouth:

"She's always so busy."

"My dad, too."

"No one sees me."

"I just want my mom."

I understood immediately what he needed. We called the parents in for a conference and we spoke about a lot of personal problems going on at home that they did not share with their son. They opened up to both the Principal and myself, but they didn't want their son to know that his mom was diagnosed with cancer and that she had to go for treatments and stay at a family's house which was out of town.

This situation was obviously a very serious one but usually when we see children coming to the office because they are distracted, inattentive or just misbehaving it usually has to do with a family situation that they need to sort out with a counselor. Sometimes it could also be stemming from a peer who is causing conflict during lunch or recess. Children just want to be heard, they want to know that someone is listening to them and helping them figure out their fears and worries. The negative attitudes and situations were taking over their day and they couldn't seem to get through the darkness. Talking to someone for a few minutes each day seemed to help but something more was needed.

After so many experiences like this, I realized precious moments do have their rewards. I needed to create events at school that would fill up families hearts and minds with positive, creative moments.

What if we could find a way that both parents and children could be together sharing in or understanding their child's curriculum or interests? What if we could create those precious moments? What if for a short time each month parents and children came together in a shared learning, creative experience? I imagined a free program provided by the school in a safe environment. We could provide food so the parents wouldn't have to worry about dinner that night. We could also keep the parents up to date with changes in the curriculum and new and exciting ways to learn the tremendous content for the school year and of course, family experiences that would be memorable forever. I believed it would be magical.

I shared this vision with the staff and quickly 15-20 staff members were on board and happy to make this happen. The past PTO President had many wonderful fundraising ideas and the staff would take care of the presentations. Monthly events were based upon a theme or content area. The staff and I brainstormed ideas and each staff member volunteered to be a chairperson in charge of coordinating the nights event for their particular month. Once we had the year covered with teacher leaders and a theme for each, the groups set out to plan. Their leadership role was very important in that they gathered other colleagues and met on their own to figure out activities, materials needed and locations around the building. Flyers were created and sent out to parents so the school would have an approximate head count for dinner, refreshments, etc. The *Parent Academy* committee would then meet a week before each monthly event to close up any gaps. Together we would walk through the evening from registration and check-in, flow of the activities, and closing up the night. Every event was an opportunity for parents and their kids to be part of a learning experience that promoted creativity and awareness. *Parent Academy* was what this community needed and the teachers and I set our minds to providing amazing events every month.

Calendar of Events

September

What do parents and kids need in September? Our first workshop focused on schedules and time management. The kids made a list of all the events they were involved in whether it be inside or outside of school. They were truly amazed at how long the list became. A monthly calendar had to have space for ONE day. ONE day to spend together.

October

October was devoted to Reading. How could Reading become a creative activity? It can if you can act out the story. Activities were set up where the parents and children moved to different rooms. It was a happy trail of weaving around and stumbling upon another creative challenge. Scrabble tiles became the gateway to finding new words and thinking about those words as ideas for a project or invention. Legos, Play-Doh, crayons stationed to get the creative mind flowing. Yes, you're never too old to experiment with Legos, Play-Doh, and crayons.

November

November was perfect for inviting in families to carve out space to become mindful of all the blessings we have in our lives. Parents and children were engulfed in journaling and drawing pictures. We had them answer questions in their journal such as, "What special time was most memorable for you and your family?" Alongside the writing we encouraged them to draw pictures of those precious moments together.

December

Just when the school year is in full swing along comes the holiday month of December where everyone's energy level and exhaustion level is at an all-time high. Why not take time out to spend time with your child? I'm not talking about making decorations or craft gifts for your loved ones—I'm talking about setting time aside to "play." Learn and play together. We set out to create Family Math Night. No, we are not going to drill facts with flash cards or give lectures on how to improve your child's standardized math scores, we are going to "play." Math games, origami, Tangrams, and pattern drawing and graphic designs just to name a few. Concepts of geometry, algebra and even basic measurement—yes, using a ruler were all present and the students didn't even know they were being exposed to this content. The parents and kids were enthralled. Musical rhythms teaching fractions. Who would've thought fractions could be so much fun.

January

In the New Year, we always offered a book club where parents could take time just for themselves after the holiday exhaustion to connect with adults and discuss their thoughts and feelings regarding raising children and living a fulfilled life. A life that they could feel confident in their decisions as a parent. I remember the year we picked *Energy Bus* by Jon Gordon. The parents left our book club feeling refreshed and had a strong handle on their thoughts about their life and future ahead of them. The session was filled with discussions and questions about people we allow "on our bus" to ride the journey of life together. We examined our attitudes towards others and ourselves. We made clear goals for our family and lives that we would live it out with a purpose. What family decisions were draining us of our energy and which ones filled our tank?

February

We added Family Fitness Night in the month of February. Many of our committee members were active. They run, exercise, and even teach boating lessons. The idea of infusing healthy habits into our lives came up as a discussion but quickly turned into creating another event. Of course we could find time to work out together as a family. Days of parents sitting on the sidelines holding the Gatorade bottles and towels can be turned into a family event. What if we could provide a night of fitness and health? Students celebrate Heart Health Awareness during the school day in Gym and Health classes. Fitness can be creative. The Family Fitness Night was a success to say the least. Families moved their bodies to music in the gym. Zumba moves, any moves as long as you kept your body moving. Smiles and laughter filled the faces of children and their parents too. Parents did not stand on the sidelines for this event. They were part of the night, part of the activities that were planned for ALL family members.

We filled the gymnasium with over a hundred parents and children eager to move their bodies creatively for Heart Health. We offered Kids Yoga in the cafe (it was cleaned and mats were provided). In the other half of the cafe the head of Food Services was sautéing zucchini and squash and speaking to us about nutrition and food choices. Kids had a chance to become chefs. Our local hospital RWJ Barnabus was on hand to give blood pressure screenings to parents and give out brochures and advice on how to keep our hearts healthy.

March

March was highly anticipated because throughout schools and libraries there has been a tremendous movement in STEM or S.T.E.A.M in our school district. Yes, Art is everywhere. Science, Technology, Engineering, Art and Mathematics has a place in schools throughout the country. Can students design, test and solve problems at hand using everyday objects like popsicle sticks, rubber bands, paper, glue, magnets, etc.? We had spaces filled with opportunities for students to build towers and bags and all kinds of fun things. Our high school students also showed up with Robots that they built. The students were amazed to see that technology isn't just about playing a video game and earning points and rewards. Students had a chance to practice coding—telling the technology which direction to move in order to achieve an outcome. Maybe helping the mouse to find his cheese by programming it to do so.

April & May

When our school art show was ready in April/May we took the time to offer parents a chance to be an artist. Parents and kids grabbed a palette, squirted the colors they wanted and went off to paint together. It was interesting to see the parents who decided to complete this adventure using Pinterest. Why are we afraid to trust our creativity that resides within us? Why must we think that our product has to be perfect? Isn't the process of creating enough? Creativity resides within us all. Trust your inner voice and your heart. Trust that your mind and imagination have the capability of greatness!!!

Making Your Own Precious Moments at Home

My time in the school, working on the *Parent Academy*, made me realize the impact these nights had on families, behavior, and academics. But I realize many schools don't offer these types of programs or opportunities. It's up to us as parents to find precious moments throughout our lives. This can mean taking some of the ideas from the *Parent Academy* and injecting them into your home life. It can also mean simply being PRESENT with your child. Wherever you are, be all there. Sometimes the smallest time can be precious. Driving in your car with your child can provide an opportunity to listen to them explaining their day, or even share in singing a song together on the radio—even if we don't know the words. Letting them know you're interested and they have your attention makes such a difference. Creating precious moments doesn't have to be elaborate or cost a lot of money. Cook a meal together, create a story—it can be silly or scary. "If we take care of the moments, the years will take care of themselves."

To make the most of your precious moments, have a few rules, that's the teacher in me . . . sorry!

Rule #1
Release all judgement.

Whatever your child is interested in will give you an insight into their hearts, minds, and dreams of the future. Sometimes we are at fault when we decide to impose our interests on them. This creates a judgmental environment where children will shut down—they won't express their creativity for fear of being critiqued by you. Let's face it, we are probably the only ones our children look to for love and safety and we never want to be the reason they close themselves off.

Rule #2
Let them lead.

As I said before, singing a song together can be fun but you can also turn into drill sergeant, curse cop, and all of a sudden the fun song turns into a lecture. Cooking a meal together can be amazing but again if you're worried about having too many carbs the precious moment becomes more about a nutritional lesson than the process of preparing a meal together. Let your child lead in these moments. By them choosing the song, the meal, the story you have something worth far more than gold.

Rule #3
Be curious, ask questions,
but not like an interrogation.

We all strive to have a good dialogue with our children, how many times have you felt like you were rapid firing questions and not getting the answer you wanted? Rest assured, they won't give them to you at least when you want them. Be patient and they will open up and when they do be genuinely and sincerely curious. Children know and they will feel your love and sincerity to make them open up even more.

If you have an opportunity to carve out more time, there are many things you can do to provide family moments that include everyone and give your children opportunities to get their creative juices flowing:

CREATIVE CUES

Planning with a Purpose

Set aside a quiet time in a space that is comfortable and happy to hold a family meeting about what might interest everyone. Listen to everyone's input and provide some pros and cons about carrying out the plan.

Putting Family First

Agree on a day in the month that works for the whole family. Look at the calendar as a family. Some family members might have to rearrange appointments or commitments. Having the courage to say "no" to get-togethers and "yes" to family time is a step in the right direction for letting your family know they are important and first in your life. This modeling will help your children understand priorities as they grow older. "Can I move this get-together to another day?" "If they are my friend, they will understand."

No Judgements Allowed

All members of the family agree to be present, to be open without judgement. Bringing together a family to discuss an activity opens up each member to have an opinion and criticize the other. The family needs to agree to state their reasons in a respectful way and to get to a point where everyone can agree to something.

For example, each family member can write down on a piece of paper, "I would like to spend the day doing _____ because as a family we _____. This will help each family member understand that the idea has to help the family as a whole grow together and be purposeful."

Responsibilities Shared

As parents we tend to take over a situation and do everything for our children. Building responsibility in our children requires us to take a back seat and let them figure out the rest. For example, every family member gets assigned a job to do to make this special event happen. Some members might be responsible for gathering the materials, creating decorations, reminding the other members, mapping out the day with a list or itinerary, packing up the car, setting the family room up with tables and chairs, etc. Depending on what activity you choose, the responsibilities will be different for each.

Need more inspiration try one of these:

◊ Cook a meal to connect with a holiday. Cinco de Mayo: Mexican Meal Plan, decorations, music, desserts, table setting.

◊ Picnic in the Park: sandwiches, bicycles, games, bring along a field guide to discover new trees.

◊ Visit a museum: take along a sketchpad, discuss favorite pieces.

◊ Sit in your backyard: take turns describing sounds, sights, and smells. Make a collage of things you forage from nature.

◊ Recreate a board game with construction paper, markers and stickers: create new characters as game pieces.

◊ Trace an outline of your child on poster board then have them trace a full body outline of you.

CREATIVITY BREAK

Find your favorite children's book, and have some fun with it! Read it with your child and then come up with your own version of it together! Rewrite the pages or create an alternate ending or write a follow up story to the book you love using your imagination! Use cardstock to create the pages, draw the illustrations by hand and write the text in crayons! Allow yourself to be silly and make a memory you will cherish!

Afterword:

HEALING

As you may know by now, creativity has so many benefits. Creativity can do extraordinary things. Creativity actually even saved my life. It healed me. Creativity is healing—it can heal a broken heart, it can help you heal while grieving, it can heal an anxious mind.

Healing My Broken Heart

Five years ago I was on a journey that would change my life forever. A failed marriage after 25 years of loving another until it hurt, of giving my heart to a person who couldn't see me for who I was, of being thoughtful and making special every holiday and birthday celebration. Years of feeling empty in a house filled with love for our children, but not for each other. Emptiness and loneliness have a way of grabbing you and suffocating you until you gasp for air.

Creativity was my oxygen.

What did I turn to when I was sad or lonely? Some

friends told me to have a drink and relax. That it would all find its way but it never did. I waited year after year for intimacy to return on all levels but it didn't. Waiting to be visible. I grew so angry that it made me a completely different person, incapable of communicating to a man I vowed to love for a lifetime. My words were hurtful and damaging.

After the divorce, I found the most beautiful shops. I learned along with others in a community of makers, or just shared my love of making with teachers, parents and close friends. Yarn shops and fabric shops held open nights where others like myself could enjoy conversation and share stories while making and creating. It would be in these places where slowly I would become whole again.

When I had to say goodbye to a beautiful home and piece of land that held memories and stories for over 20 years, I took with me boxes of everyday items. I also took with me my son's memories of childhood. Their trophies, cute outfits, handmade blankets and quilts, and of course their framed artwork. When I look back at their artwork I can see that they had insight to themselves and the world before we could ever imagine what journey their life would take.

One piece of art was a painting of a large umbrella. My son, Gregory, felt the need to put our home underneath that umbrella. He painted it yellow and outlined it in black. Usually artwork only has the artists name written on it but my son wrote the words, "Home is protection." Yes, he would be the one to study marketing and advertising in college. Did he know back then that words and visuals were important to him?

Sometimes we forget to just be present in that moment to celebrate the small words and drawings that make our lives meaningful. Finding those pictures again reminded me that his creative spirit was alive and well and pure. He dove into it with splashes of color and large strokes of paint. He was fearless and confident. He wasn't aware of any critique because he didn't see the world as one that would criticize him or vice versa.

Rummaging through more memories as I cleaned out my attic, I found a self-portrait that my younger song drew in 5th grade with a fine point marker. At the time the art classes were involved in artwork that could become a fundraiser for the school. Students created a picture and parents had an opportunity to buy that picture on a mug, a blanket, notepads and anything you could imagine. Of course his grandparents wanted his special drawings and keepsakes.

Sitting in my living room packing my memories away I stared at this picture and couldn't believe that his drawing was him as a young man of 23 years old. It looked just like him. His drawing was of a young man with spiky hair and a beard. Of course he didn't have a beard in 5th grade, but he depicted himself. He told me how much he always wanted a beard. Going through puberty his body and facial hair was growing faster than his classmates. He also grew as tall as 6'3". Basketball was his life as a young boy and he eventually fulfilled his dream of playing basketball for his college. After freshman year, I went up to see him to visit and watch a game and there he was with a full beard. I immediately thought of his artwork. Did he know back then? Can our minds tell us things before we could even imagine it?

While packing up the memories of my children I also found my drawings from the past.

Creativity Heals Us as We Grieve

Several years ago, as the school year was settling in and we were diving into the learning, I received notice early in the morning from the Principal. The mom of one of my students collapsed at the kitchen table as her daughters were getting ready for school. She died suddenly without warning. Some of the class parents already knew as they were friends of this caring woman who suddenly was gone. Like an earthquake this news shook everyone to the core. This tight community, along with these students and their families had been together since Kindergarten. We all went to the wake and waited for her to return back to our class when she was ready.

The school psychologist's office was conveniently located right next to my classroom. My heart hurt for months upon end. I didn't know what to say or do for this beautiful young girl. When she returned to school the class was happy to see her but knew they had to be gentle in helping her acclimate back to the routines of the day. Sometimes in the middle of the lesson she would come up and ask to see the school psychologist. But most of the time all she wanted to do was draw pictures. I would give her the time and space to do this.

I allowed her to draw at her desk, my desk, the reading corner and anywhere she felt comfortable. We all felt the pain and we didn't know what to say or do. What we realized was that we couldn't say the perfect thing or do the perfect thing to help take away the pain.

But all of us, the teachers, the parents, the students were present. We were present and truly listened to her stories about her mom and the memories she would tell us. One day she came up to me and showed me her red delicious apple and said the apple smelled like her mom. "Yes, your mom is everywhere", I said but my heart knew that that apple had been part of the many fruit baskets delivered to the funeral home. My heart ripped apart as I tried to think what I can do or say. Her perfect world had been turned upside down. Being present in the moment is the biggest present you can give anyone. And the drawing, the smell of apples, the storytelling—these were all healing acts, and at the heart of them, they were creative. Her dad, family, friends and school community supported her emotionally and academically. Today she holds a Bachelor and master's degree in Sociology, helping others with their struggles.

Creativity Heals Anxiety

When I went through a very difficult time personally, I was being told to look up and stay positive, but it was the creative moments I would spend drawing, painting, knitting, sewing or anything I would make with my hands that got me through these difficult times. I know I'm not alone. We hear today of many people suffering with anxiety and depression. According to the (ADAA) Anxiety and Depression Association of America, 18% of the population in the U.S. suffer from Anxiety disorders. It is the most common mental illness in the U.S. affecting 40 million adults. But what about the children? The ADAA also reports that anxiety disorders affect 25% of children between 13 and 18 years old. Research shows that untreated children with anxiety disorders are at higher risk to perform poorly in school, miss out on important social experiences and engage in substance abuse.

Where does creativity fit into this?

Everywhere you go today there seems to be magazines and self-help articles on fighting anxiety or depression: "How to Recognize Signs of Anxiety." "Ways to Cope with Anxiety." "Five Easy Steps to Relieve Stress." "Foods to Help Fight Off Depression." At the same checkout counter there's always a coloring page book. Instead of reading about ways to fight anxiety, just get out those boxes of crayons and start doodling and creating. Soon your anxiety will disappear. Creativity will tug at our heart strings to wake us up so we can enter into a world of calm. Art can also help us understand children who might not be able to communicate their emotions or thoughts using words. Art can help children self-regulate themselves, by calming their body and mind down especially if the art is sensory based (Play-Doh, clay, finger painting, etc.).

Creativity certainly heals as I know this all too well. I took to knitting in the beginning and it seemed to heal me in ways I couldn't have imagined. Every stitch was a meditation and a prayer for healing. Every stitch made me forget about my worries and fears and soon I was not only losing myself in the practice of knitting but I started to dream about my own design and pattern. I thought about what the stitches would look like if I changed the pattern. I made samples and ripped it out. I jotted notes and found charted pattern books of famous motifs and designs. I searched for just the right color and played with bringing in different colors and designing it on graph paper. My imagination and creativity was exploding. I soon worked out all my anger, frustration, sadness until it started to change. I felt free and full of hope. I felt a sense of rebirth. My prayers were being answered for my designs and thoughts were now turning around.

I designed a knitting pattern for a cowl called, "Blossoms by the Beach." I had test knitters test the pattern and it was published and placed on Ravelry for all to enjoy. My years in high school dabbling in fashion design classes were a distant memory until they resurfaced as a way of showing me that my creativity was still alive inside of me. I wasn't late to the party or too old, I was tapping into my creativity to heal myself through difficult emotional times. It took me two years to feel whole again and back to myself. I realized that I wasn't the only one who was healing because an art form presented itself in difficult times. My free and creative spirit was alive once more.

I promised myself from that point on that I will never suppress it again. So I embrace new creative learning experiences whether it be in knitting, sewing or painting. I accept challenges and will not run away from it because I can't seem to find the time. No I will make time so that this creative spirit will live in my soul forever. I am truly alive each and every day now that I make room in my life for "making." How do I do it?

I have designated a small space that is filled with bins of yarn, as well as fabric so I can sew. Paper, markers, scissors, crayons, paints, and boxes of embroidery floss that are ready for me to dive in to use. There's a peg board above my sewing machines where I can hang inspirational pictures and ideas. To the right of the small narrow window is a framed picture that reads: DREAM BIG * use kind words * SAY I LOVE YOU * LAUGH * GIGGLE * be silly * TAKE A MOMENT TO BREATHE * TRY NEW THINGS * BE GRATEFUL *

Oh, how powerful these words are. They stir my creative side, calm my anxious side, and just give me permission to be the me I know I am.

How Deep and Miraculous This Creativity Is

I want to leave you with one final thought. I believe creativity can work miracles because creativity is a gift from God. And God works through our making to remake us when we need it most. I have seen this countless times in classrooms, in my own home, and in the world around me. Now it's your turn to take the keys I've given you, and the miraculous healing creativity offers, and go into the world around you with an open heart willing to create and make in oh so many forms—from poetry to stitches, photographs to painting, it is all there just waiting to be unleashed.

Acknowledgements

It's funny how life sends you on a journey that you truly cannot see where it will all lead. I did not have a plan to write a nonfiction book on creativity, but I did know I had something inside of me that needed to be shared. I had a creative response to a tough time in my life, where I intuitively felt the need to create. I intuitively knew the "making" would heal me, and that difficult time led me to this place, this reflection of seeing creativity and its potential to bring JOY to everyone and everything. Speaking from my heart, living with my heart on my sleeve, and trying to figure it all out, the stories and results of infusing creativity into my daily life and the lives of my students created this book. It literally just poured out of me when I started to share my journey, and so sometimes unplanned things are the best things. I am so grateful you picked up this book, this piece of my heart, and are right beside me on your own creative journey.

Jenn, my publisher, coach and friend. Thank you for believing in me and getting this message to the world. You're an angel living among us, for you see the stories that heal us, inspire us, and then you set them free into our world. We are forever changed by your presence—professionally and personally.

Mom and Dad, thank you for believing in me and giving me my creative space. Your love and support over the years made me who I am today. Every difficult turn, every choice that took me in another direction was embraced with a loving and positive heart. You always made me feel like I could tackle the world and I'm still amazed at how far I've come.

My art teachers that I had as a child and an adult, WOW! Your work inspired me and continues to fill me with endless thoughts and imaginative play when I'm creating. Thank you for bringing beauty and color into my world. For helping me remember and trust that it's okay to look at life from the eye of an artist.

My grandmothers Josephine and Pauline who brought sewing and fiber art to my life as a young girl. Your skills and knowledge transferred themselves across generations, and I feel lucky to have embraced them and given them life again. The sewing, knitting, and fiber community are a beautiful bunch of caring people, natural and organic in their way of living. They give me hope that the world can be simple again with each stitch. We are truly woven together.

My dear friend Regina (ReRe), I loved everything about my childhood because you were in it—by my side—laughing, giggling, and fearlessly tackling all the awkward, middle school, teenage moments together. Who would've thought I could do back handsprings, cartwheels, and roundups?? You were an awesome teacher! It doesn't matter the amount of friends you have in this world, you just need a few and I'm so happy we are still close to this day!

My piano teacher, Regina (ReRe's mom), who brought classical, pop, and holiday music to a whole new level. My love of music and life would not have been the same if it wasn't for your beautiful, loving and encouraging words. My piano still remains in my life as a go to for happy and sad times, spiritual songs, and it would be a void in my soul if I never learned from you! Thank you for sharing your love of music and life with me! So many treasured memories that I will never forget.

To the students in my classes over the years who taught me how to be childlike—to forge forward into the unknown because it is where pure learning begins. Danielle, Andrew, Diane, Alexandra, Dylan, Rebecca, Ridhima, Sydney, Althea, and all of my students who still keep in touch with me to this day, I am honored and humbled to be part of your life. I still read all of your letters and look at your drawings on rainy days.

To my Toms River family who taught me to be a fearless leader while still remaining compassionate and sensitive to the educational community . . . Dave, Marc, Debbie, Cara, Estee, and Matt. Thank you for letting me be me! My teachers, supervisors, and support staff who I have worked with in the past and present. Every creative experience and memory of finding that beautiful teachable moment lives in my heart forever! So glad we are on this journey together.

My Holmdel friends and neighbors who showed me how to navigate through a world of parenting, sports teams and our everyday life commitments. We made it through and continue to count on each other for each chapter of our lives . . . JoAnn, Rosanna, Paula, Toni, Connie and Mary. Strong women who held each other together through it all!!

My Max Challenge group (5:30 Freaks), you always raise my level of workout and my body and mind feel renewed after being with you all . . . Joanne, JoAnn, Donna, Lance, Anthony, Mike and Denise.

To my brother, Thomas, who taught me as his big sister to keep believing in myself and leave the light on when life gets too dark! I love all the moments we spend together and our boys are bonded together forever!

To my sister Paula, as the oldest I looked up to you and followed you and your friends everywhere until you taught me to rely on myself and be who I was meant to be. Today our friendship and love for each other is stronger than ever. Love our early morning conversations as we drive into work—therapeutic and inspiring!

To the man who picked up the broken pieces and made me whole again with his loving and caring ways. I've never met a person who loves unconditionally with his actions and words, never asking for anything in return. You are a treasure, a diamond in the sea of life. Thank you for never giving up on me and being by my side. My Tony! My Boopy! My Best Friend! My Love!

Finally, my sons Gregory and Gerard Philip . . . you are my world. Gregory, you came into this world curious as ever and I will always treasure our talks—way back when you were a kid and still today. We always find a way to inspire each other, illuminate our ideas and dream of a better tomorrow. Continue to take in all the beauty and knowledge this world has to offer. Gerard Philip, my gentle giant, my son who is mature beyond his years and a true leader in every way—whether it was on the basketball court in college, at your job or within our family. You give us strength and help us remember the unspoken words, "Be still, it will all be okay." My love for both of you is endless. Remember to be present and enjoy each day. Love one another! That's all God asks of us! My proudest moment in my life will forever be when I became your mother.

Connect with JoAnn Nocera
and Follow Her Creative Journey

Website

http://joanncreates.com

Instagram

@joanncreatesdotcom

Email

joanncreatesdotcom@gmail.com